High Shelf

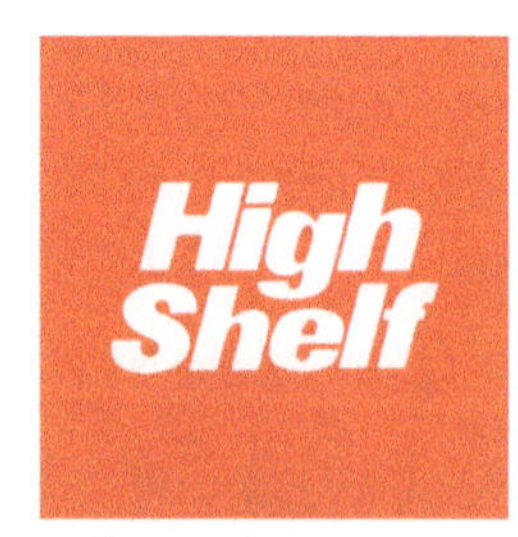

High Shelf Issue XX. July 2020.
Portland, Oregon.
Copyright 2020, High Shelf Press

ISBN: 978-1-952869-00-6

Cover Image by Gillian Loop
Design and Layout by C. M. Tollefson
Edited by David Seung & C. M. Tollefson
With Special Thanks to River Elizabeth Hall & Kristin Howe

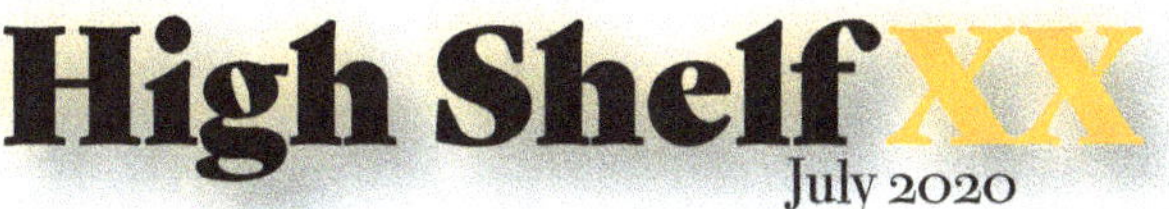
July 2020

"I was sure the whole plane ride
that I would die. If you were gone

what next bad thing? I ran barefoot
to make my connection, arrived... "
Laura Hetzel

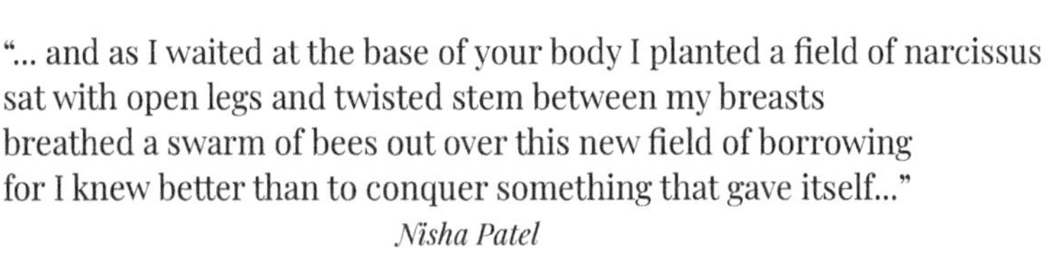
"... and as I waited at the base of your body I planted a field of narcissus
sat with open legs and twisted stem between my breasts
breathed a swarm of bees out over this new field of borrowing
for I knew better than to conquer something that gave itself..."
                              Nisha Patel

Table Of Contents

Coming Home Is So Sobering

Alfredo Arevalo

I walk in, and he's dead again;
five shots never blurred anything,
only screamed in double entendres,

encouraged bodily precipitation.
This building stands still, still
violent. A shot I never heard

reverberates, a quake resonates, this body
I thought I could read like a novel—
unusual quiver; this thigh, these nerves

never whisper goodnight. I wish I knew
every cell, but you can never know yourself
wholly, only in holes—my pores speak,

shout louder than any smile,
these teeth get exhausted hiding—
this grin was raised in familiar sin,

familial sin. I try to celebrate
my scars and creases; I can't cheer
loud enough. I search for a reflection

in a ravine—confide in corners,
castrate an unspoken dream, cast away
another because the white walls wailed.

I hold one of three old tokens:
shoot it into a mounting pile of "tails"—
converse with the next dirty piece of gold.

what becomes of us

Nisha Patel

when I bled for you, the stars trickled down my legs,
wrapped themselves around fragile bones
that once snapped like song-bird necks
my tongue watched as the hot liquid left my body
and made a home of the scorched grass beneath heel
dove into the roots of a sapling
that stood in the place we last kissed
and you had once showed me how to embrace the dirt
with a full and curious face
move the muscles of my mouth around
a soft bud, nurture it wet and gentle
and emerge with burrs smeared across my *nose*

and as I waited at the base of your body I planted a field of narcissus
sat with open legs and twisted stem between my breasts
breathed a swarm of bees out over this new field of borrowing
for I knew better than to conquer something that gave itself
so willingly to the gaze of the sun

and years later, when you finally came down from the leaves
cocooned in green and dripping with your new wings
I pressed my palms to your cheeks and said
I love you like it was all we'd need to meet the new dawn
together.

Motel 6 Rendezvous

Vijay R. Nathan

We played endless online Scrabble games.
I was your only hope on the East Coast.
The sun was up at midnight in New Mexico.
No surprise; I was particularly good at screwing.
Midnight was screwing up New Mexico.
No sun was particularly a surprise.

The sun was up at midnight in New Mexico.
No surprise; I was particularly good at screwing.
You just like to swim around me.
Sometimes, I also enjoy going against protocol.
I also enjoy going around me, just like you
to sometimes swim against protocol.

You just like to swim around me.
Sometimes, I also enjoy going against protocol.
We played endless online Scrabble games.
I was your only hope on the East Coast.
Your only games are on endless hope; I was played.
We coast the East online.

We particularly played hope games, screwing protocol.
Enjoy the East Coast, just like me. Only you
swim against the endless New Mexico sun. I also
was up at midnight going around online.
Sometimes, your Scrabble was good, to no
surprise.

pinmatik | Rocky Cape

Brandon Edwards

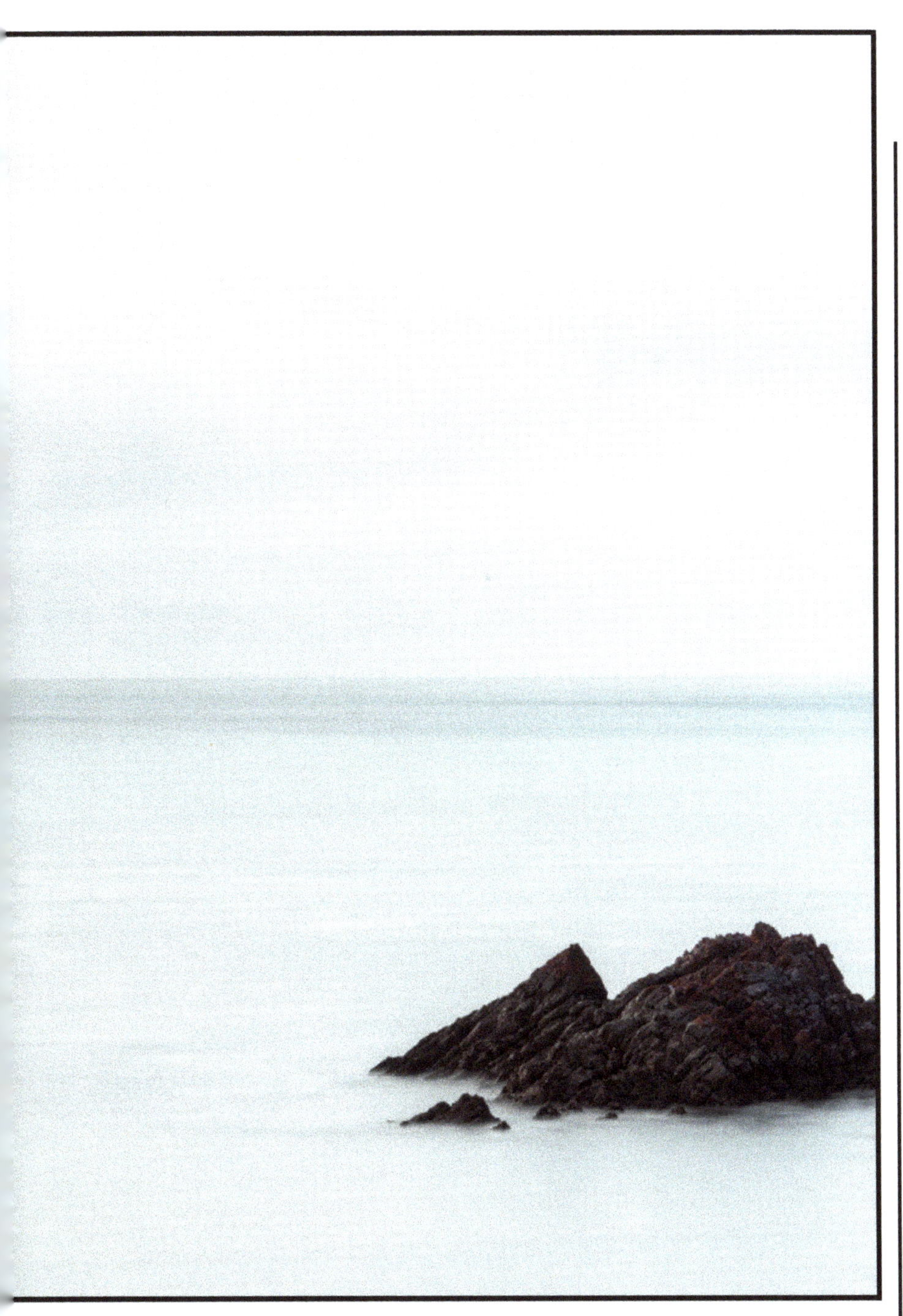

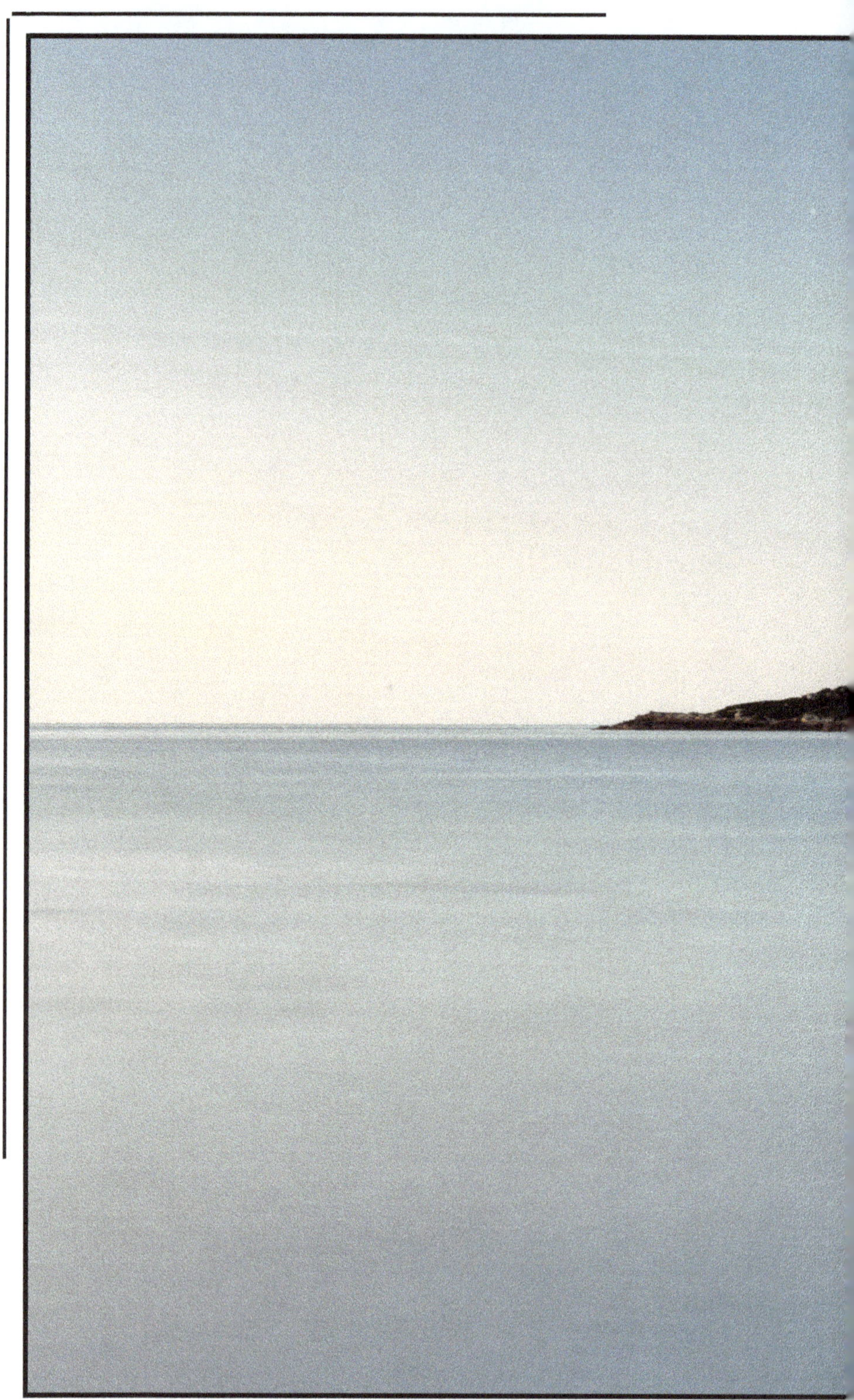

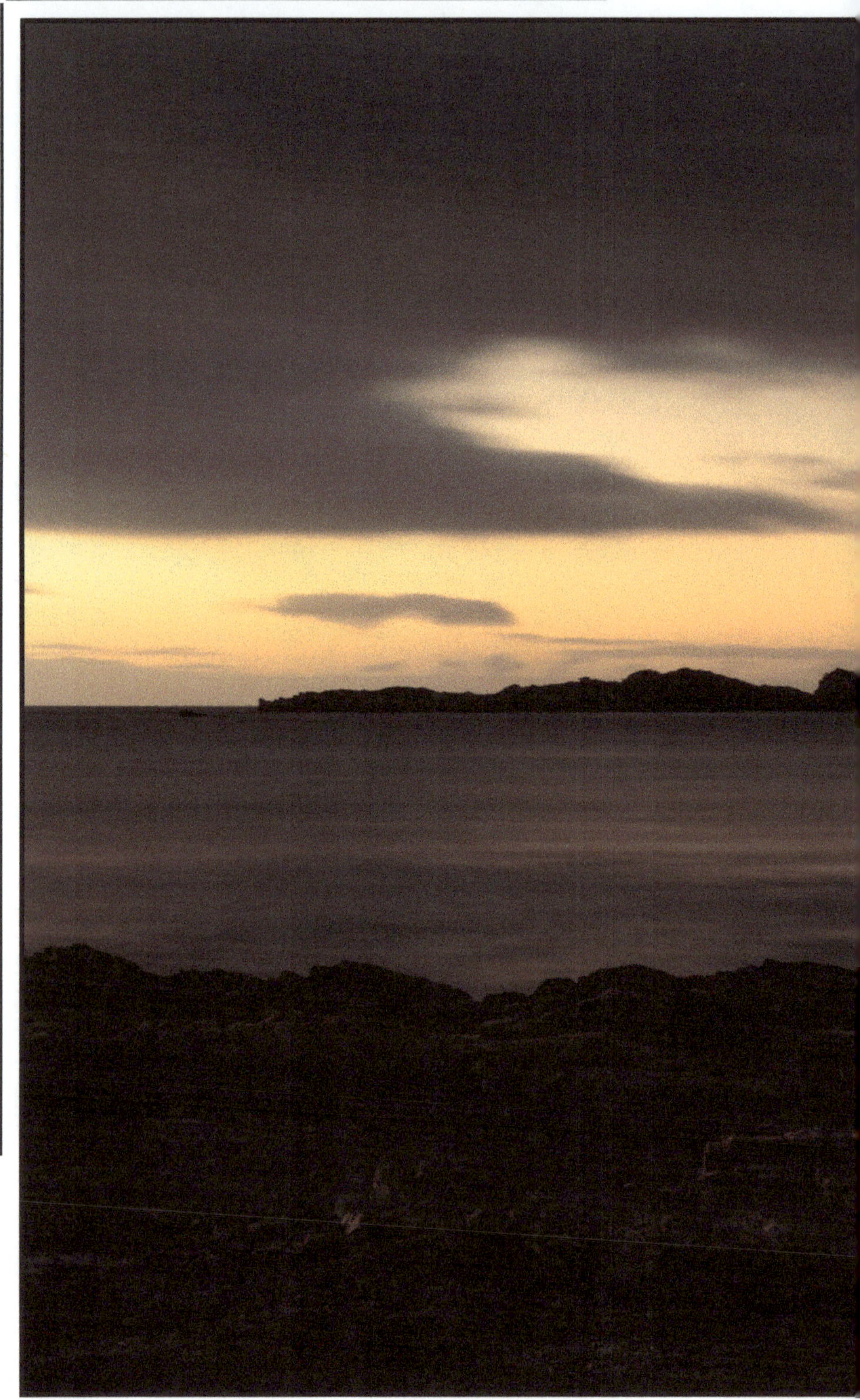

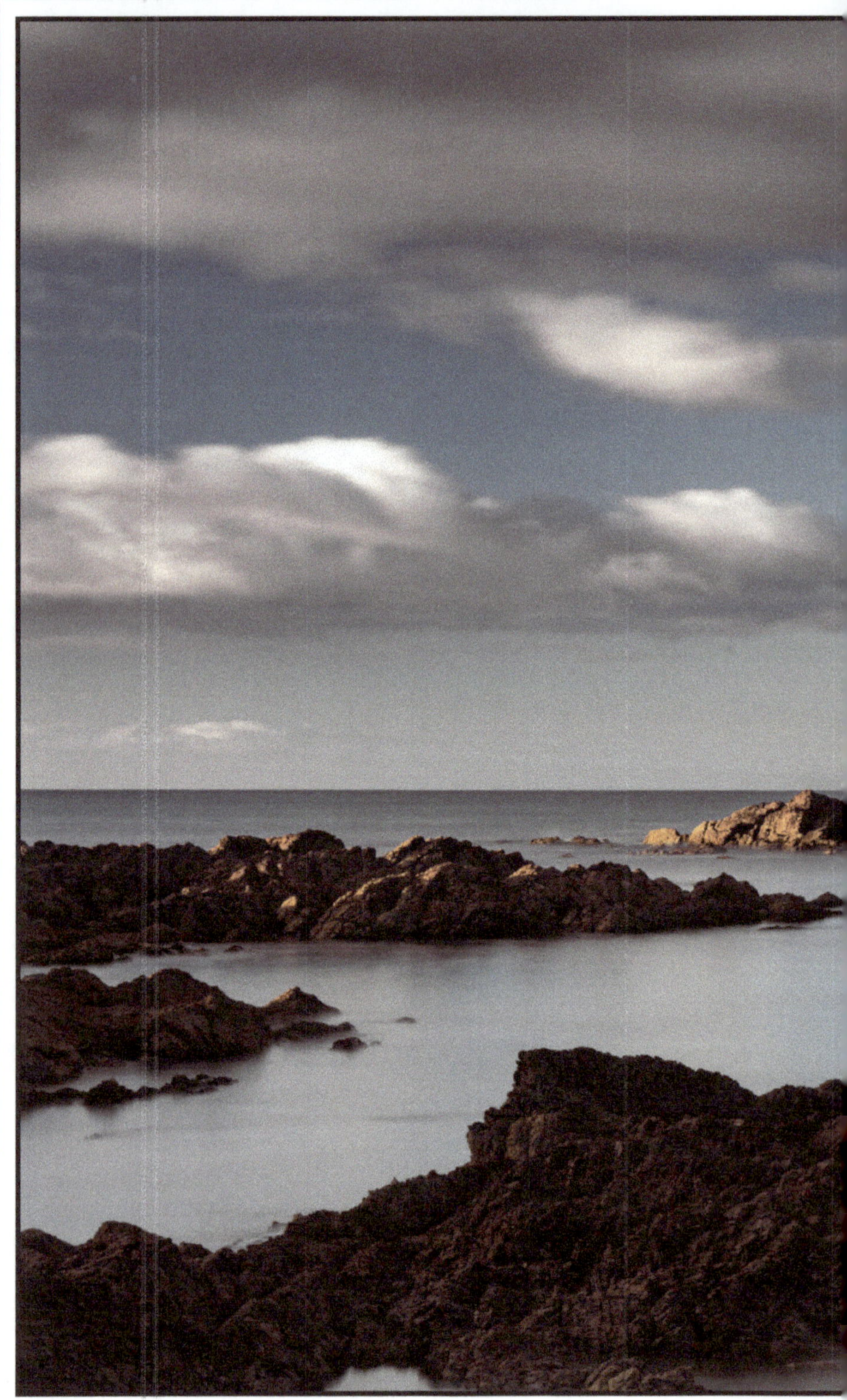

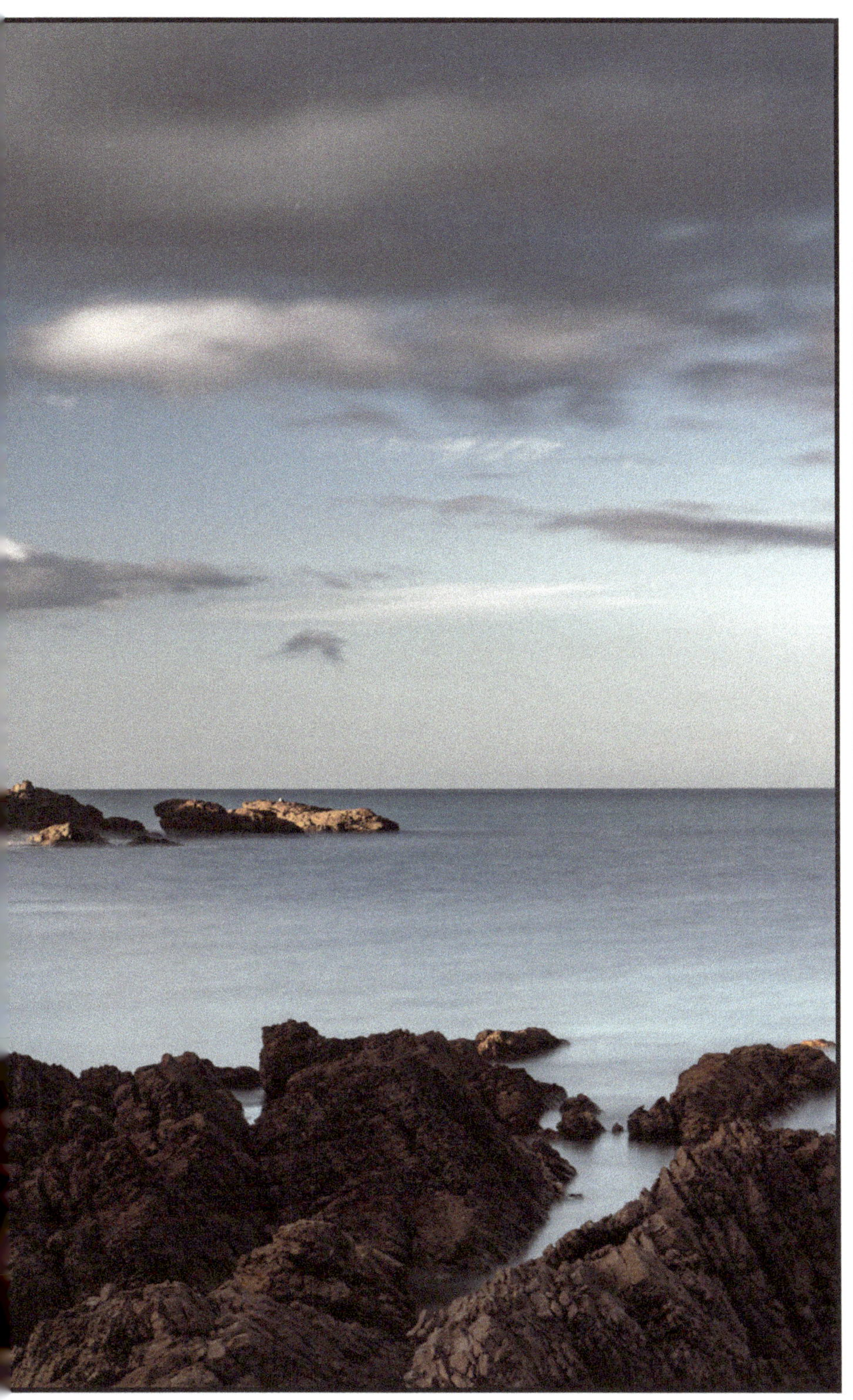

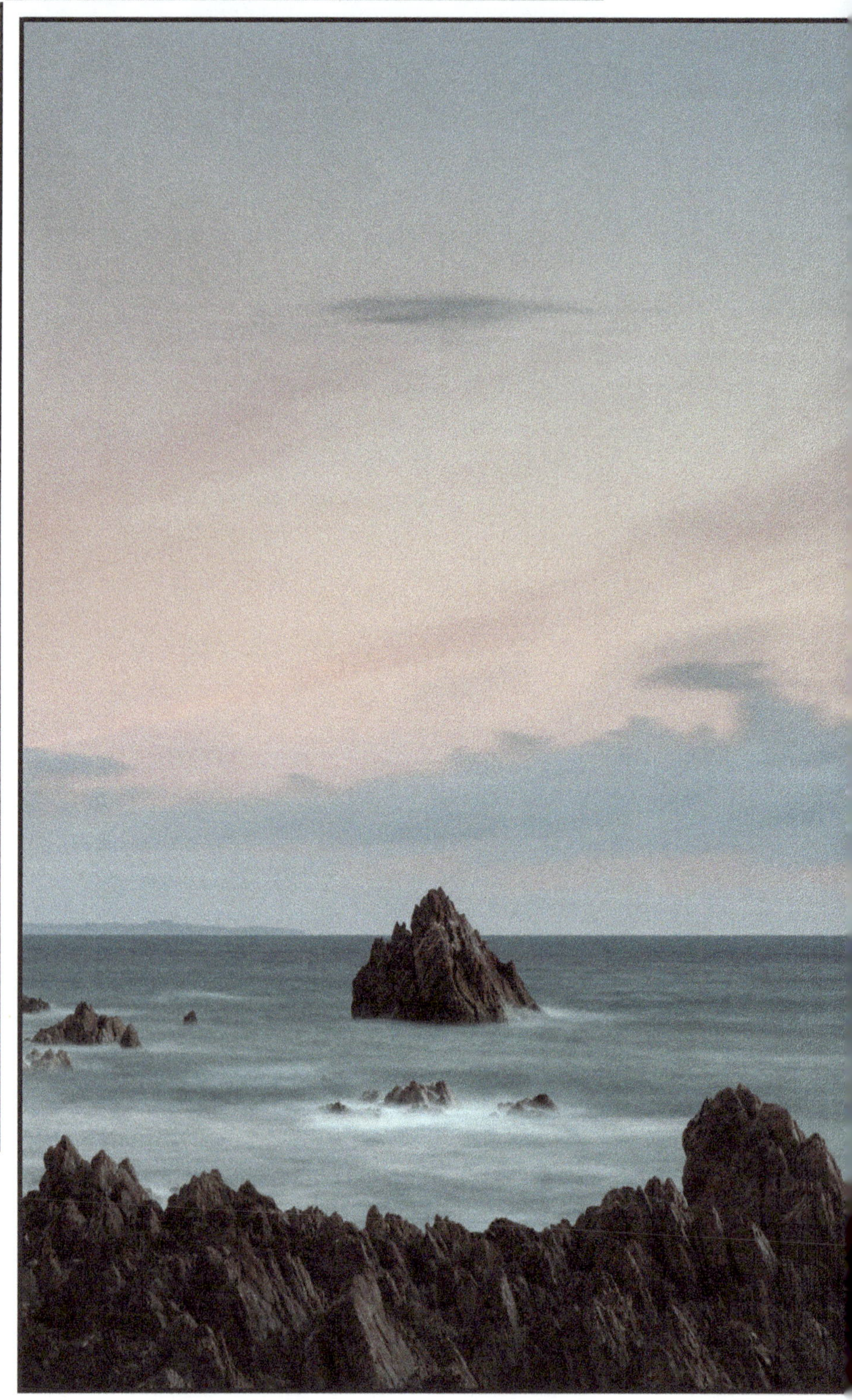

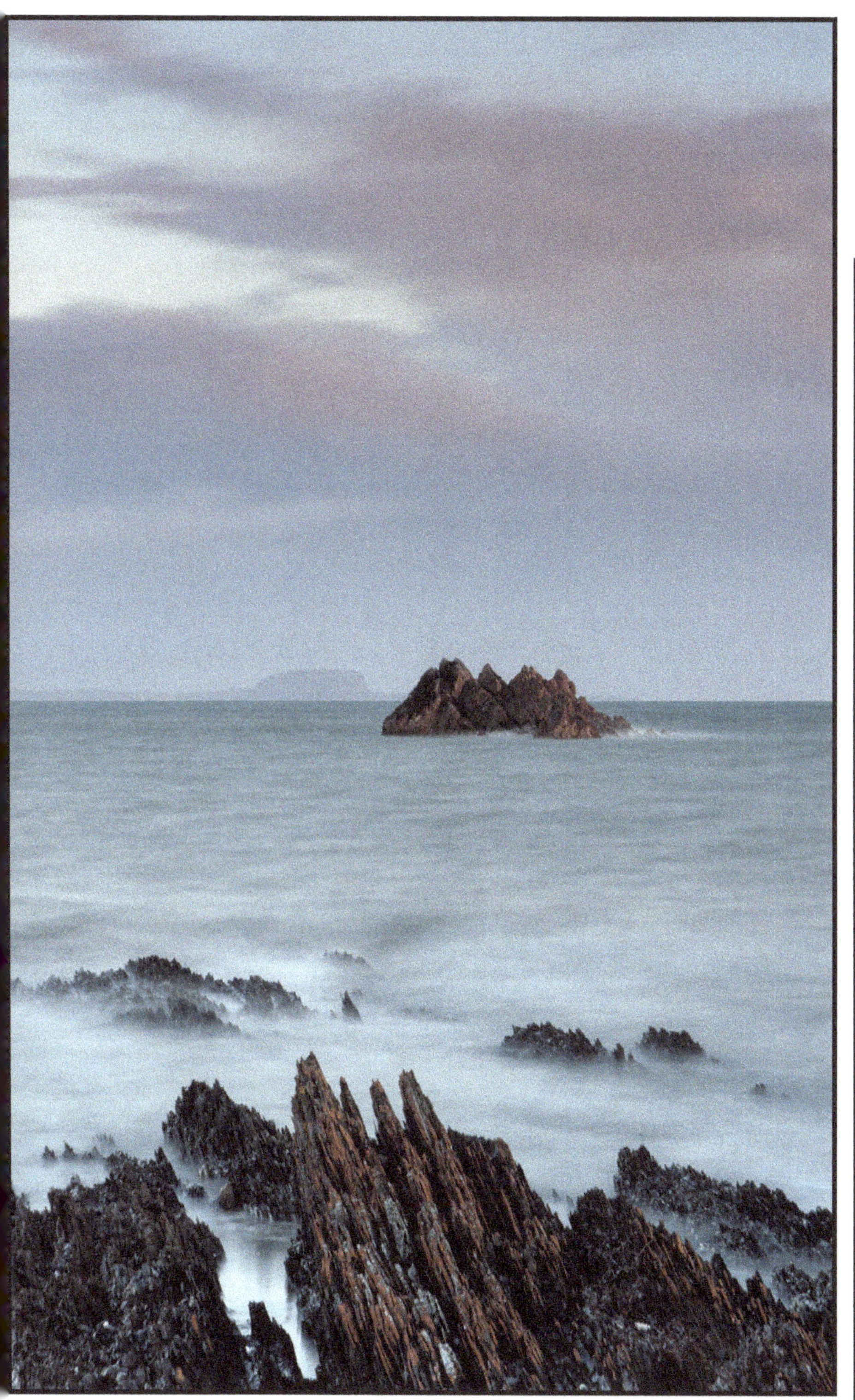

Holding Space I - VIII

Abigail Markov

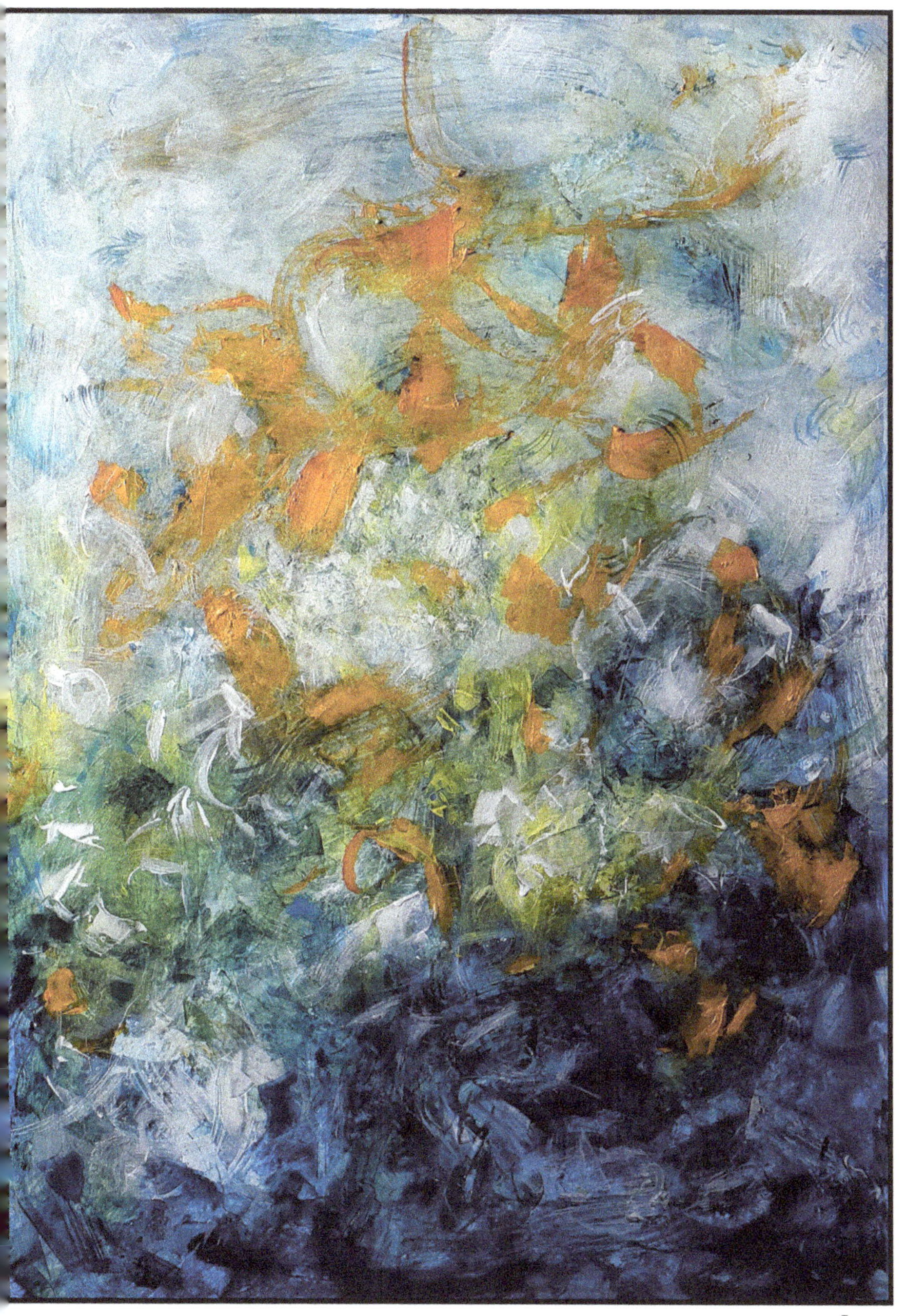

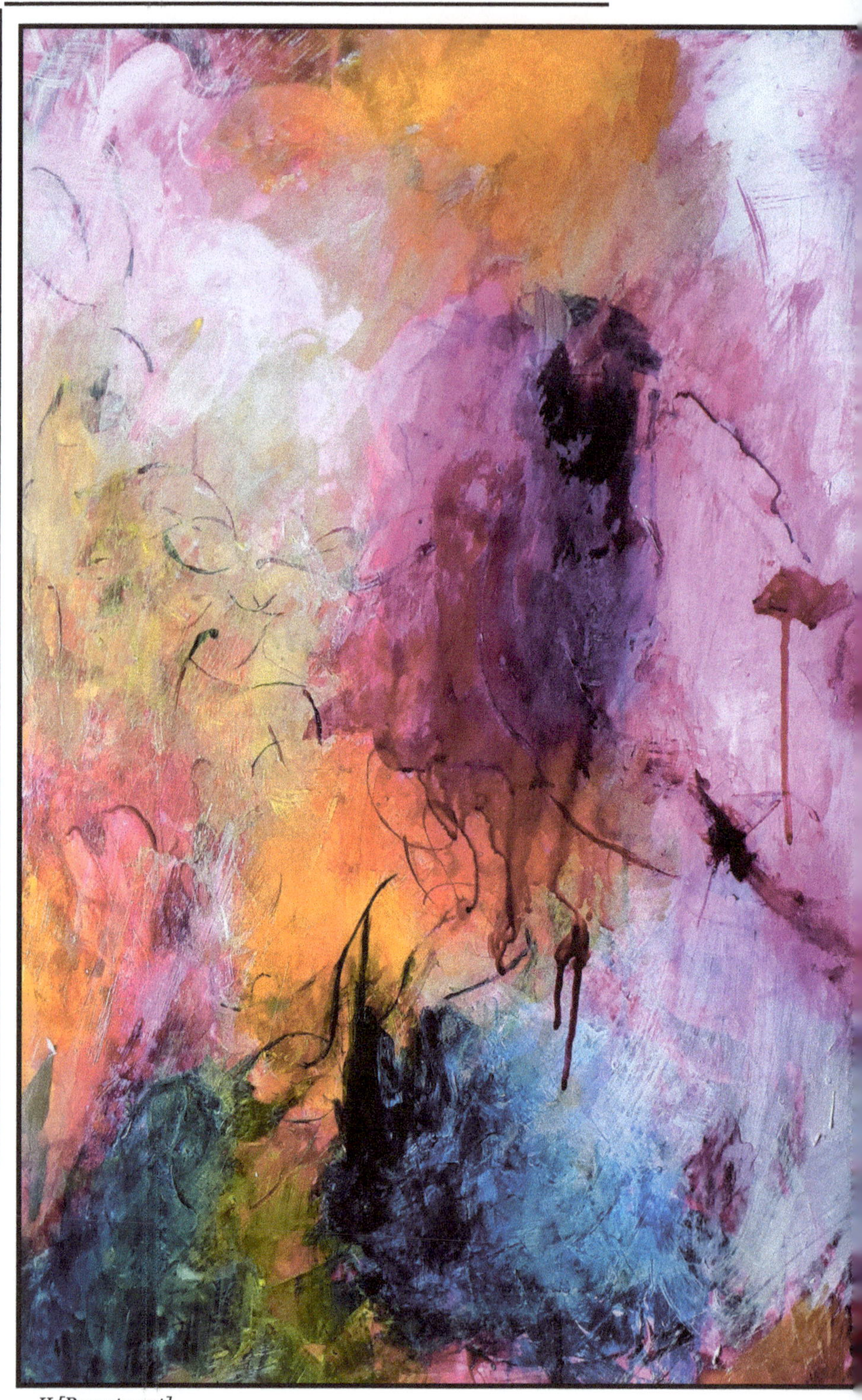

II [Resentment]

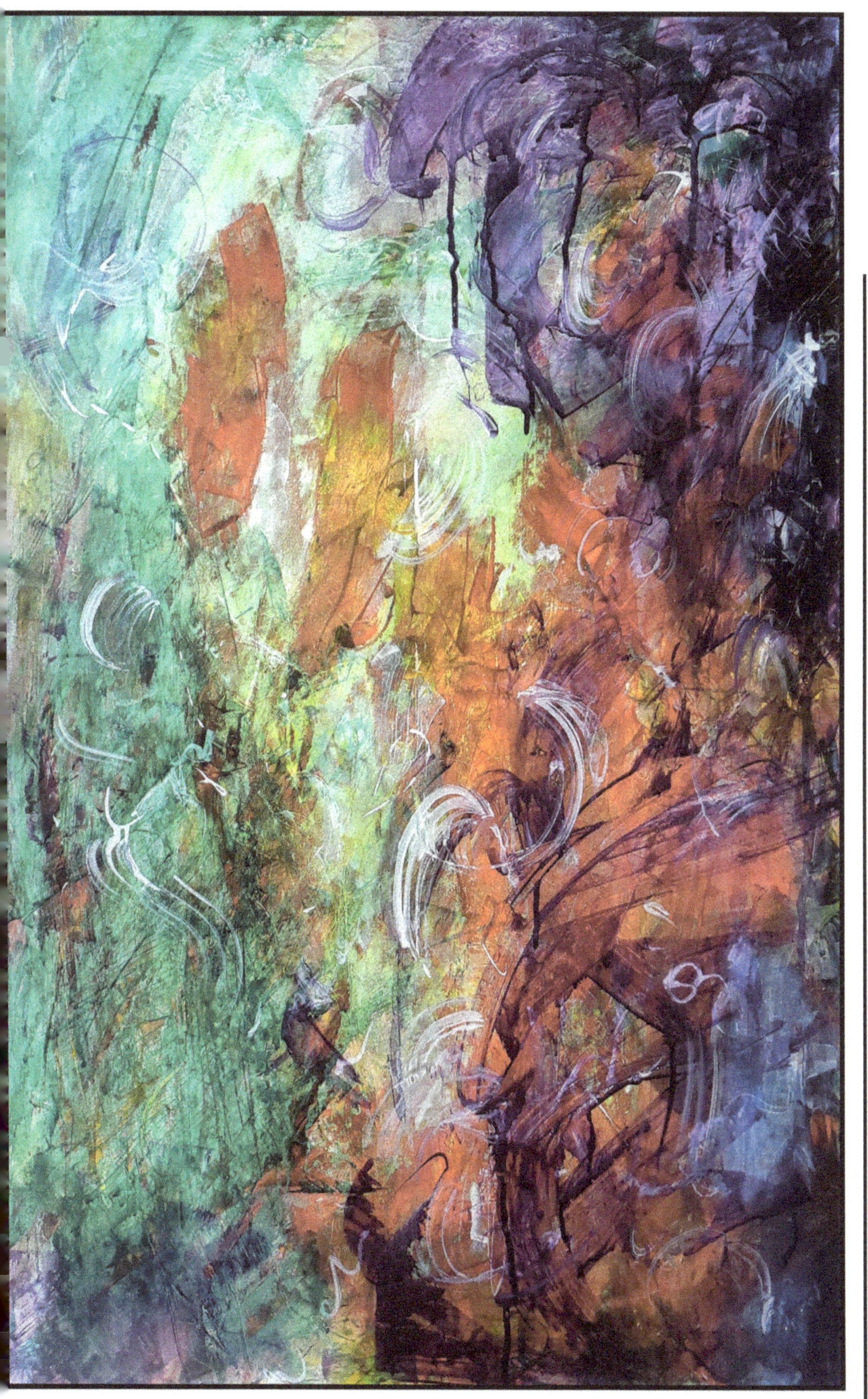

III

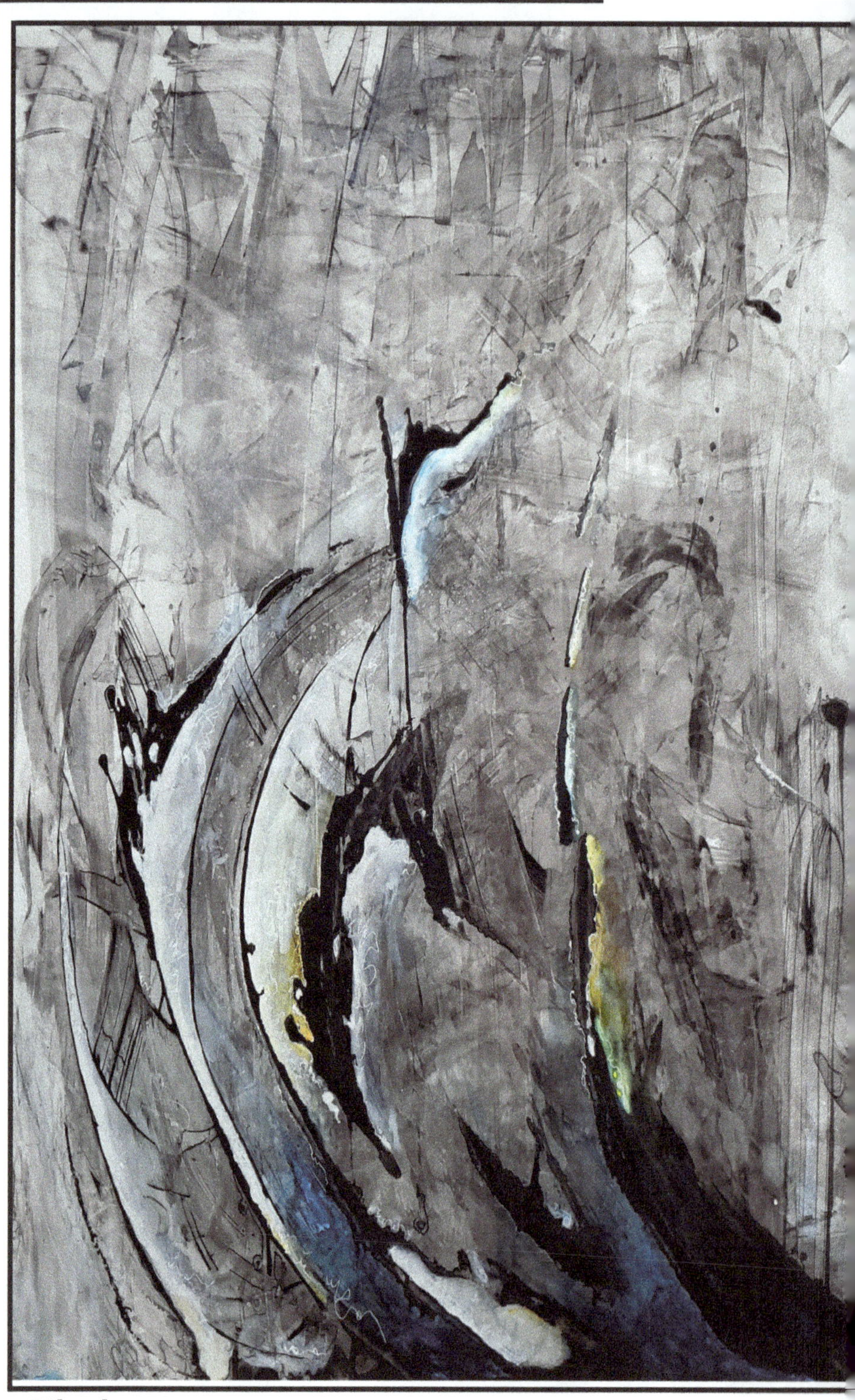

IV [4am]

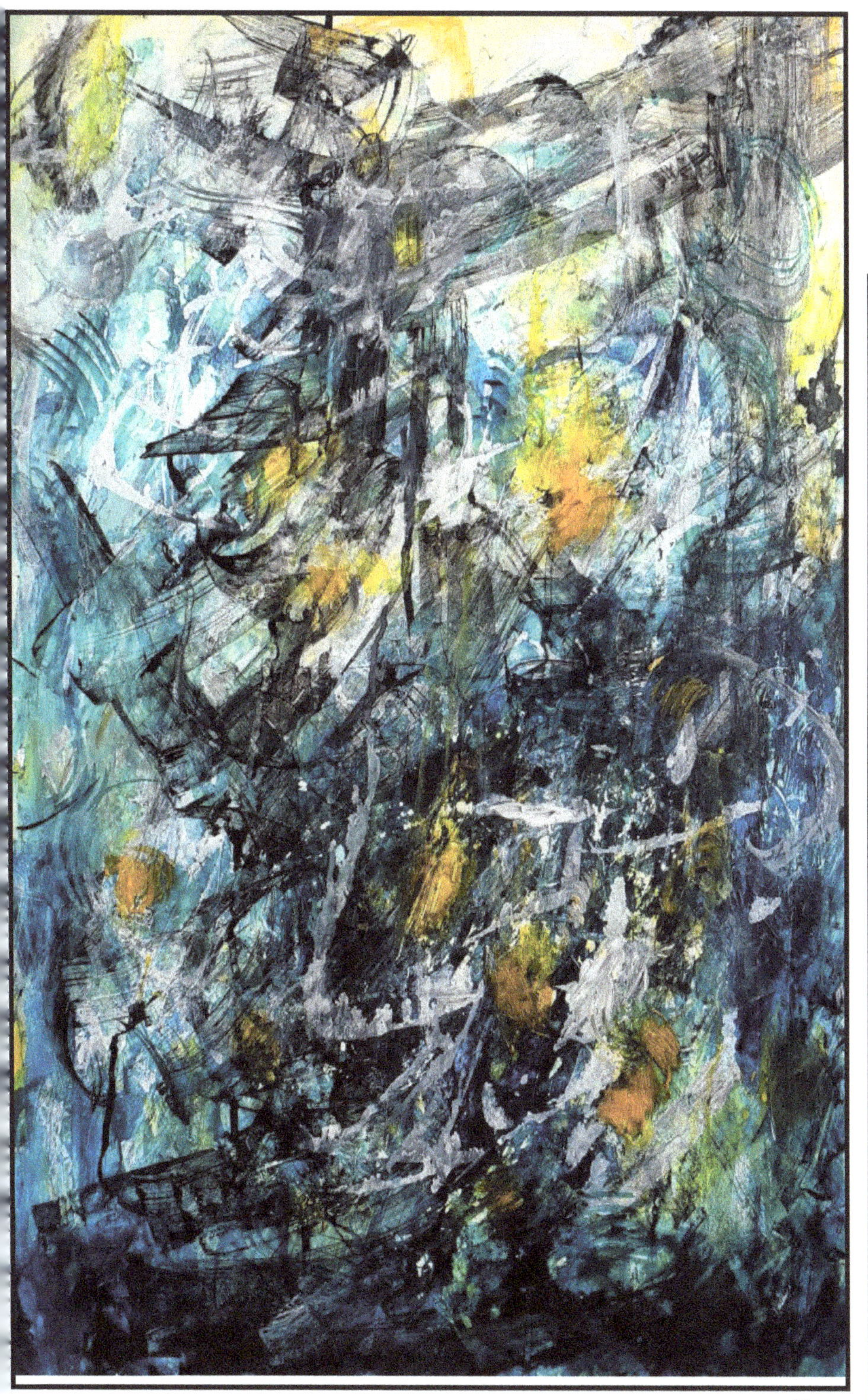

V

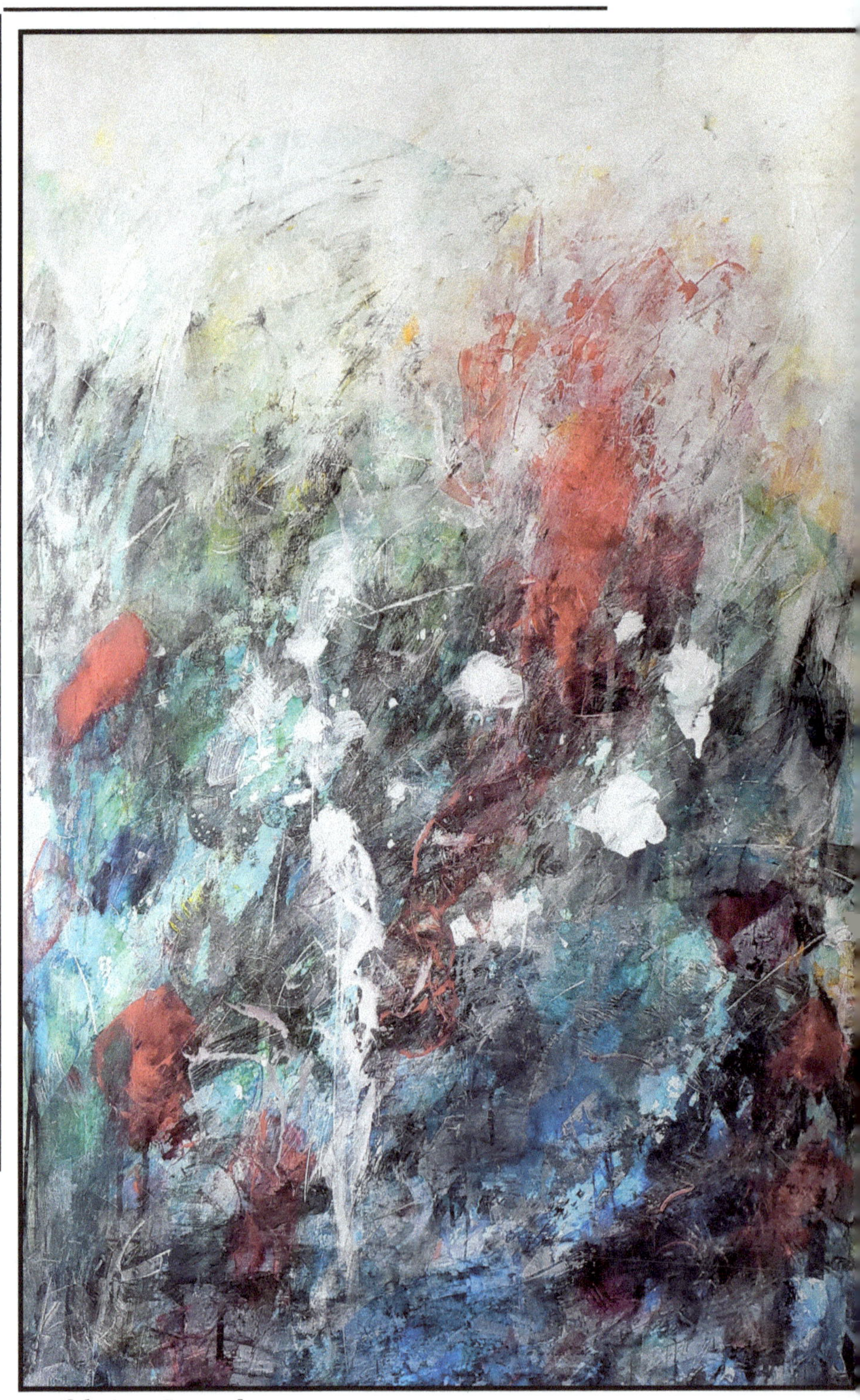

VI [The Space Between]

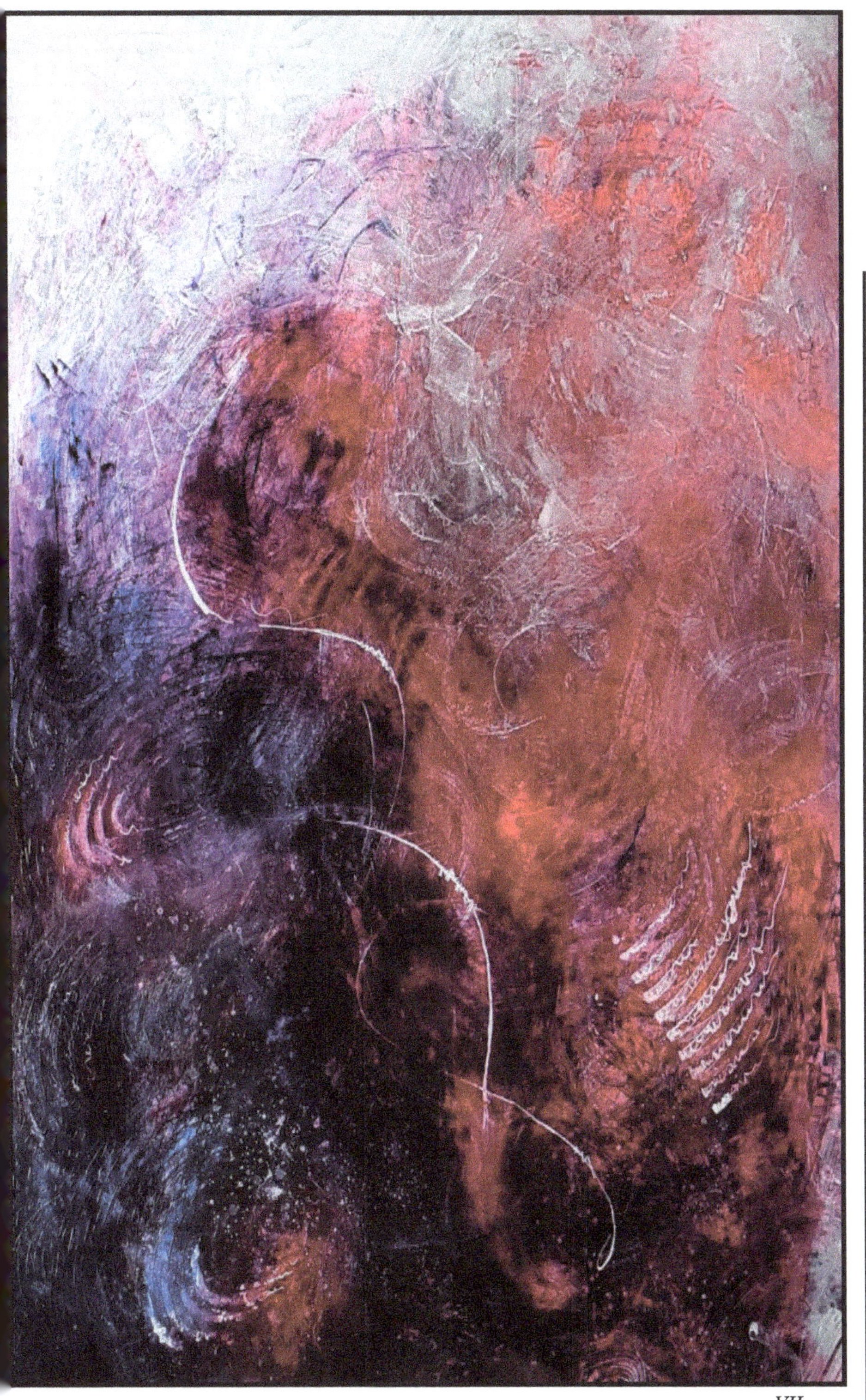

VII

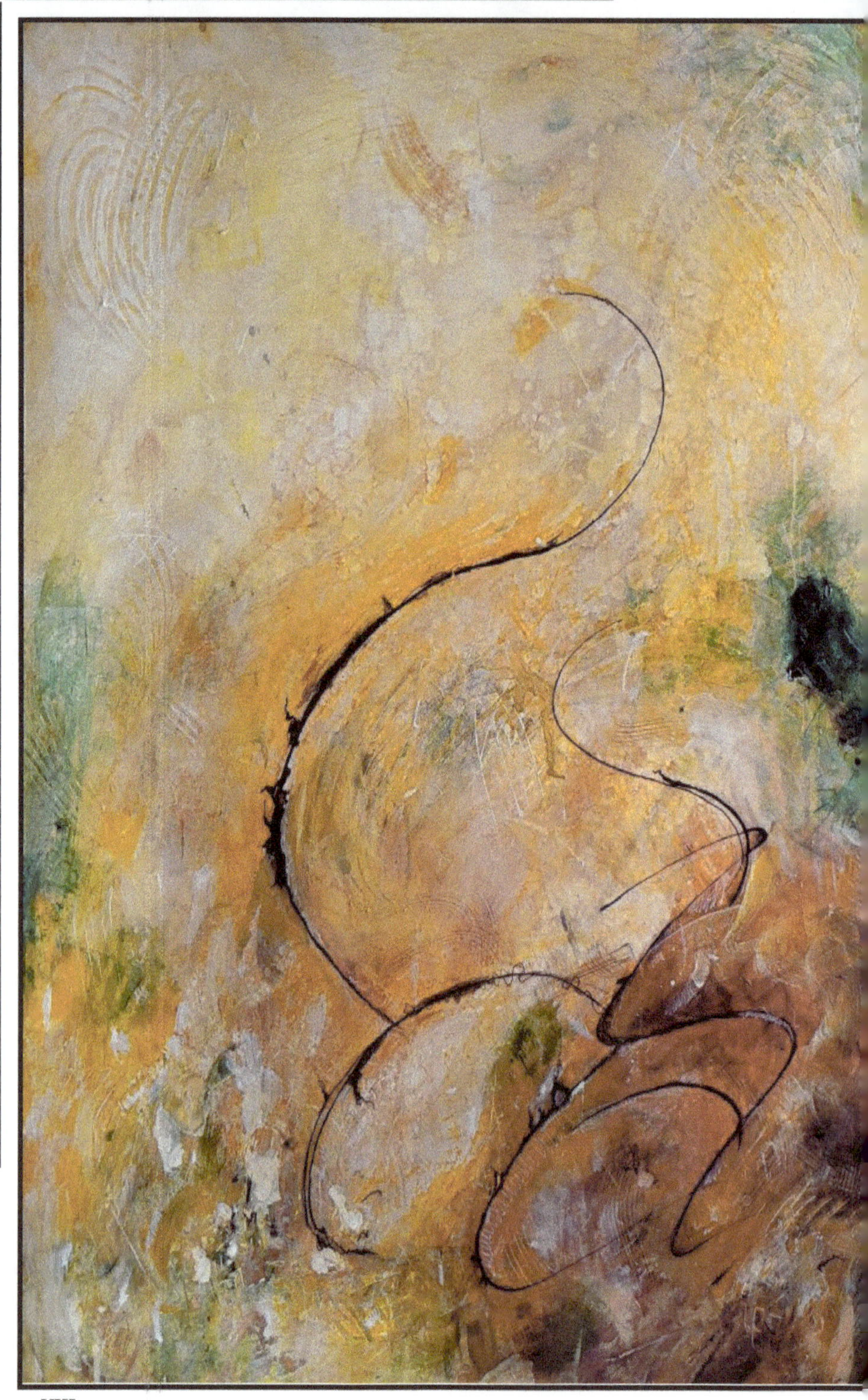

VIII

Grounding

Laura Hetzel

I was sure the whole plane ride
that I would die. If you were gone

what next bad thing? I ran barefoot
to make my connection, arrived

breathless at my gate
to a round of applause.

I learned later that you walked barefoot
to your death, barefoot

over one mile of black top
barefoot over railroad tracks

past yards, over loose rice,
people's driveways, broken glass

barefoot over all the things I know
are on that particular stretch.

All these days later
I can still feel the bars

of the moving walkway
at the soles of my feet

the bite of it that woke me
from some haze, the sharp breathing

of a sprint. I've imagined some connection
in me trying to reach you, and you

obscured. All the electricity in you
building, or leaking out.

Handkerchief

Michael Hill

My grandpa was a handkerchief man,
not sure I ever saw him use a tissue.

When he felt a sneeze coming on or
if it was just time for a good honk,

he'd reach into his back pocket and,
like a magician, flash a bright bouquet

of floral print fabric, quickly tend to
the matter at hand and then, as deftly

as he conjured it, make it disappear.
He was a tidy sort without much need

for anything he did not already have,
and he even tied a handkerchief onto

his bald head when he pulled weeds
out in our garden, one loose corner

lifting gently in the breeze like a leaf
or a petal on a flower as he blooms

once more here in the warm sunshine
of memory, perennial as the summer.

"Self-Capturing"

A. Pikovsky

A little shadowplay

       by the gardenbeds—

I thought you'd catch me by the flowers,

           with your arms dangling.

I filled the space by kissing the bark-eyed earth

             & in return, it let me sleep.

In the sun's golden glow, I trapped myself

      in a knotted unravel, resting in the dining mirror, sweating panic & swallowing.

it was the social capital of self-capturing

         the fleeting reverb of acceptance.

Ghost Americana

Nikolai Sergei Razumov

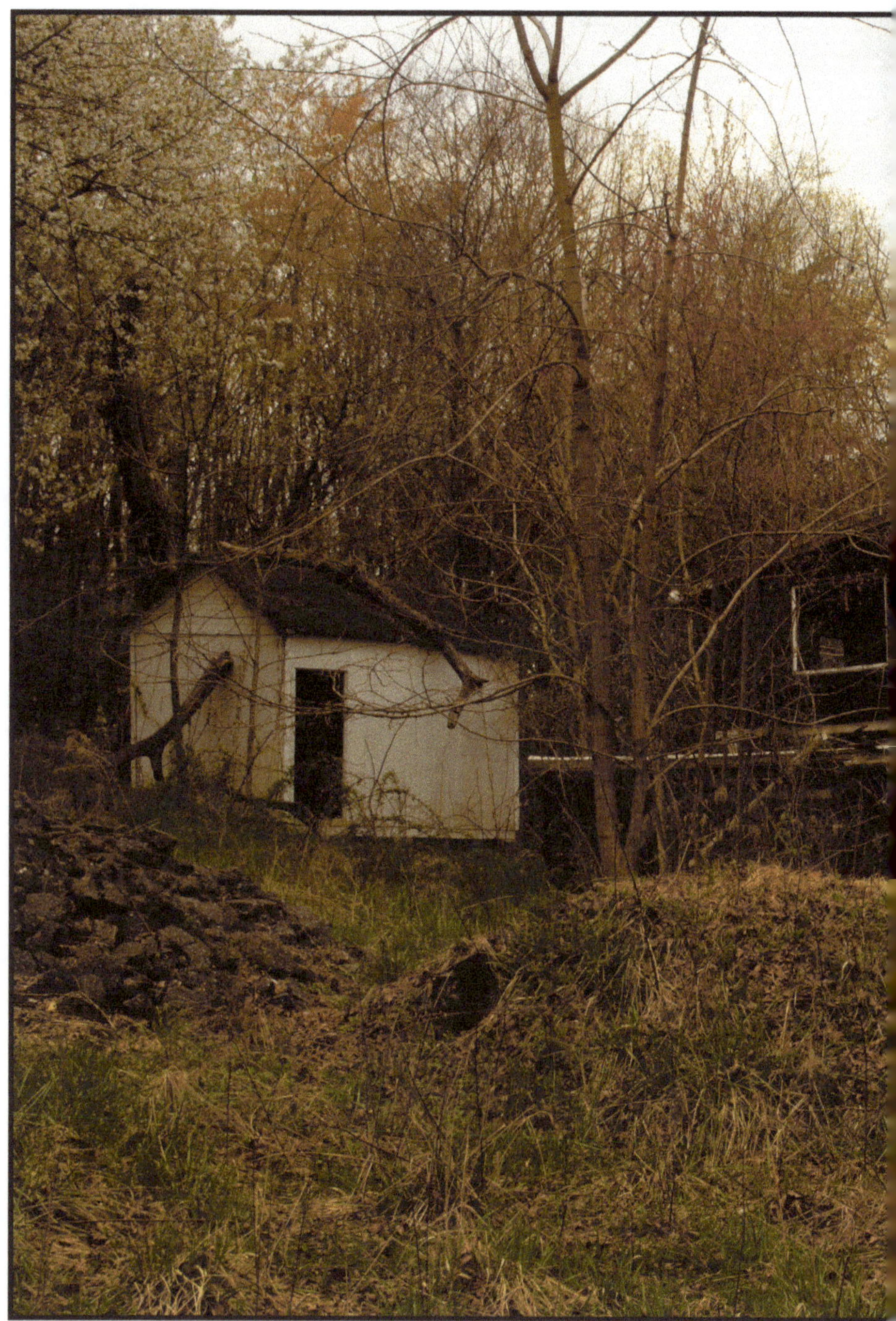

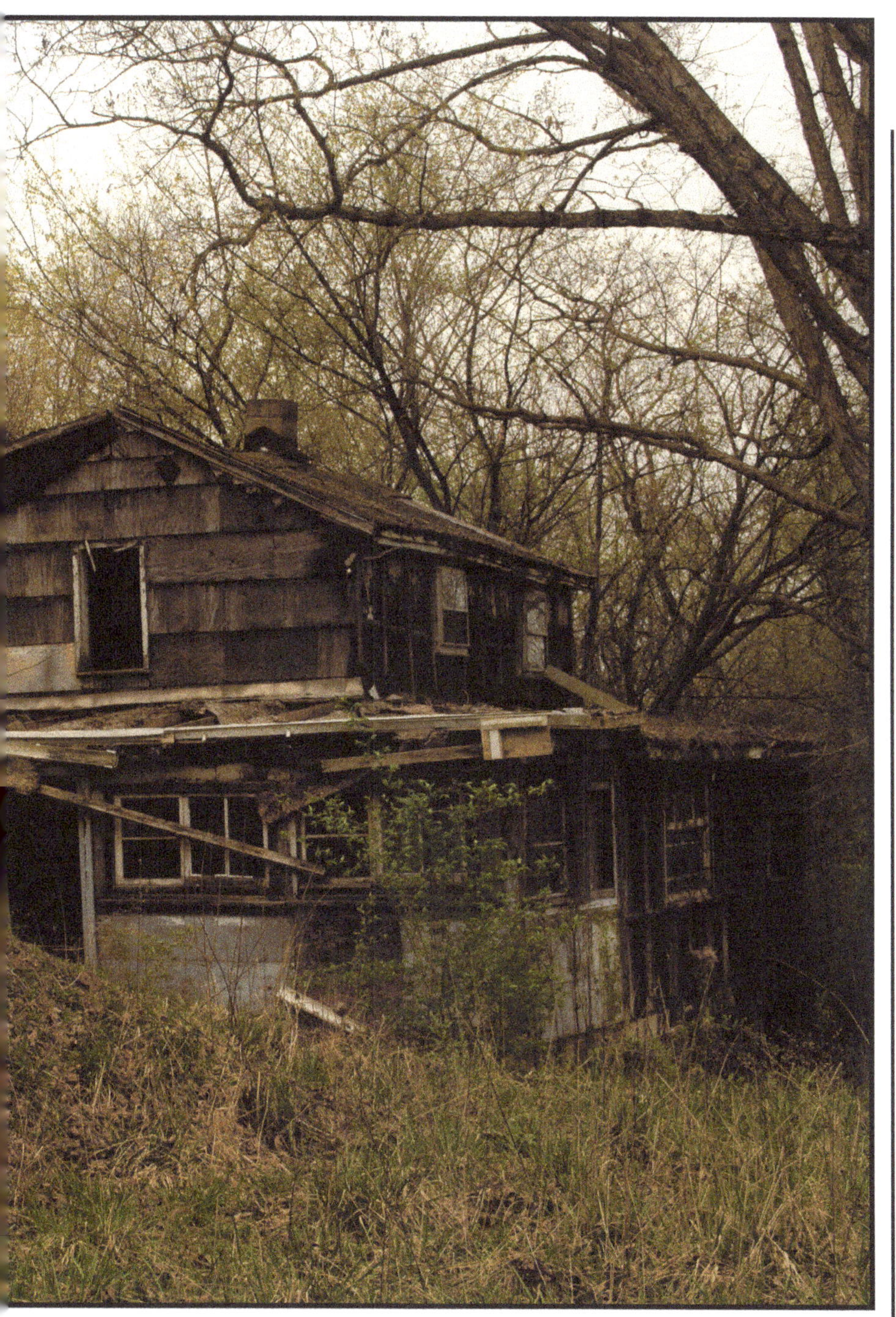

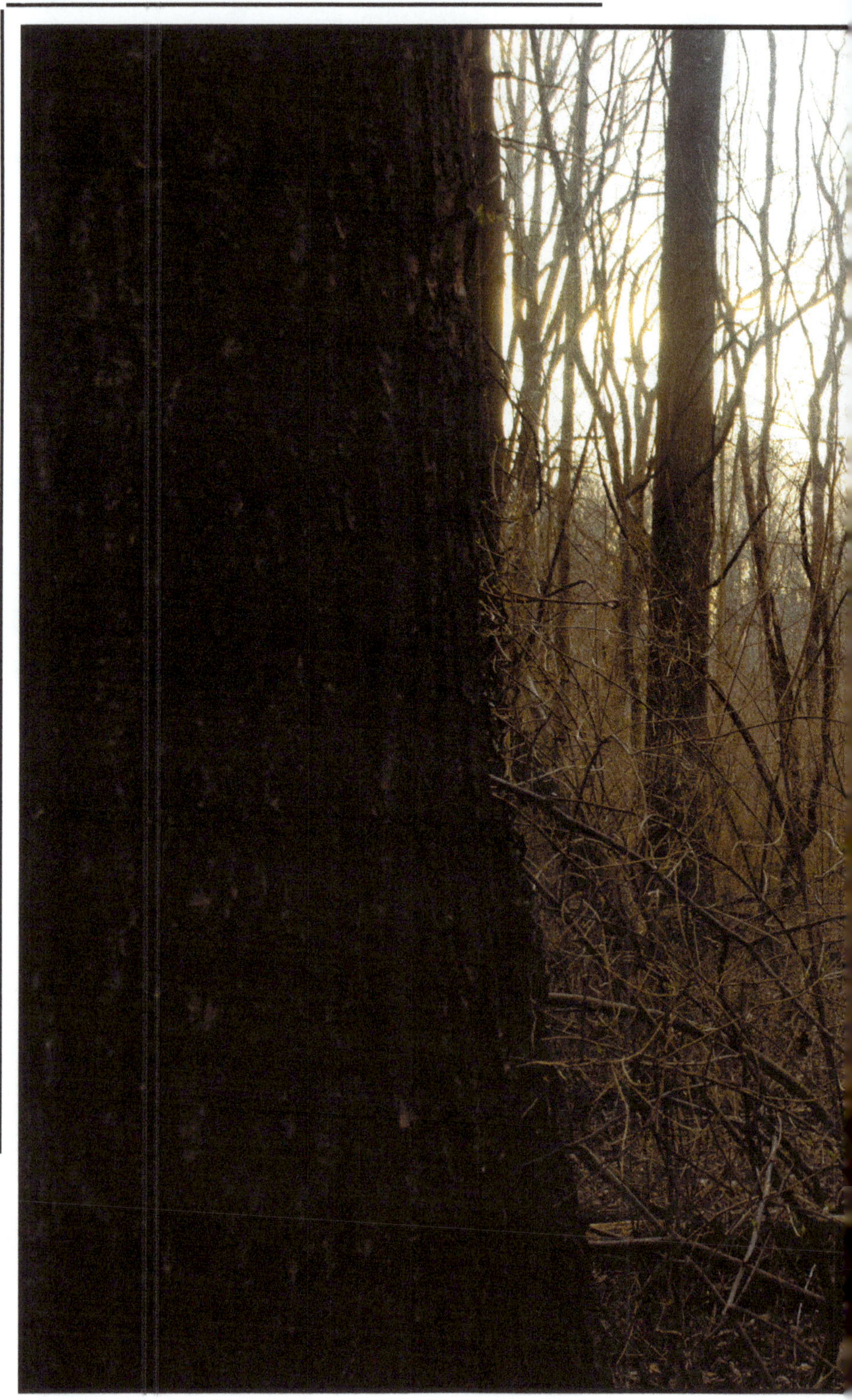

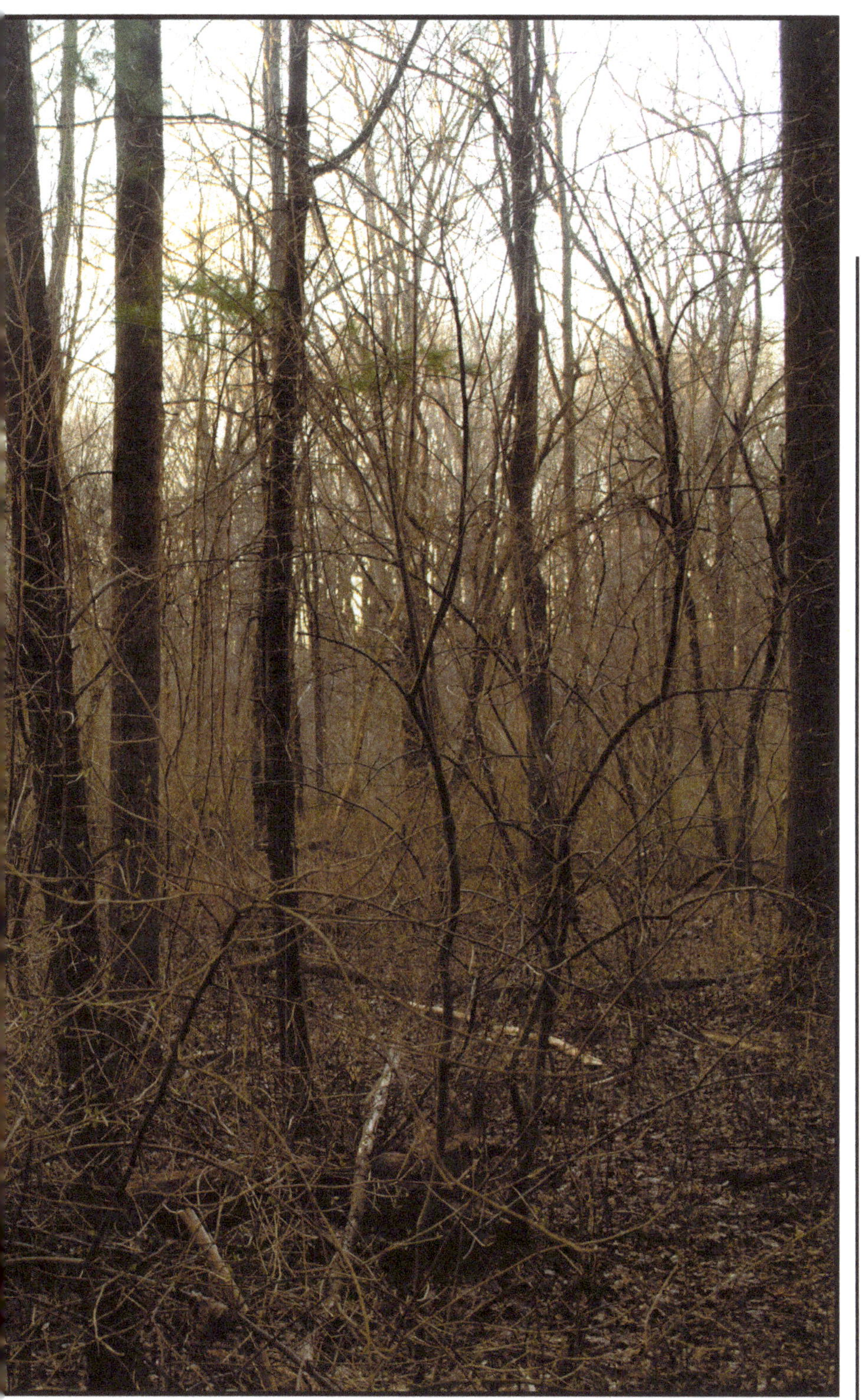

The Witch's Bridge

Elizabeth Brewster Thomas

Down the path by
the needling creek,

past its delicate
dirt-colored veins,

the unspeakable
spot like a damaged

memory darkens
afternoon. Here

we lived, under
the slats, pointing

our sticks up toward
shuttered lines of sky,

toward the soft, pale
feet of the innocent.

This mud-damp dimness
is the secret I wouldn't

tell; though we could prick
their soles until they bled,

that summer we squatted
silent, gloating in our

deadly perspective. Often
I played alone, the water

a gloss across unyielding
earth, the bridge leading

nowhere but
my swollen heart.

when I'm not easier to be played on than a pipe

Elidio La Torre Lagares

madness can hardly be feigned after the pills—the smokes—
the rum—the spill over—that wenge table—this black ashtray—
the unamused phone—Hughes' Crow—silence—not silence—
the loneliness of middle age pasta—the white couch—the cool
cat chasing spiders—the moonglow—my heart lows—the hi-hats
lazy—the inside of my chest blown like breadfruit—I slumber
slide into a deep thick—a bird and she's a city—or a cemetery—
she appears and looks at me—the golden bright eyes—the sharp black
beak—top hatted and lean—oblivion is a screensaver turned
on every three minutes—the wills—the chokes—the mill
over hell where my beautiful nothing hatches lies
besides poisoned blades and white chickens

Pedagogy

Lonnie B. Hodge

I want to be
witches knees and elbows
roots just high enough
above the ground
to stumble deep into a child's
imagination forever.

I want to be a breeze
just strong enough
to move the leaves,
and not silence the birds.

I want to be the loneliness
in the center
of a foreign pine seed
dropped from some kid's pocket
and have everyone wondering
how it is I came to be there.

Indigo

R. J. Keeler

Color of old, coldest ice beneath
new-fallen snow, fathoms deep,
has bought every purple berry
to smash into a fine bone plate,
to stain floral china darkest blue.

A plant—unlike the rest—its smallish
rough green pod to burst
along a slack, medial seam,
to gape its anatomical splay.

Cuff intense, this purple light
streams across a dyer's hand,
explodes a native virgin sheet,
stamps blue tints on warp and weft;
a fictive handshake not undone.

Until a war begins, the dye is ours.
So covet trades that keep the flower
violet-pink and meters-tall; milk
its leaves, cook an inky paste,
lend to ancient clothing looms
who'll blue impress a lass's blouse.

A violent blue assaults the hurt;
the stain's not the stain for long.

Love for the tiny blue bush, love
for the stain that clots and covers,
for the rift that rectifies the blaze;
and lastly, for the root that bears.

Drawings

Julie Blankenship

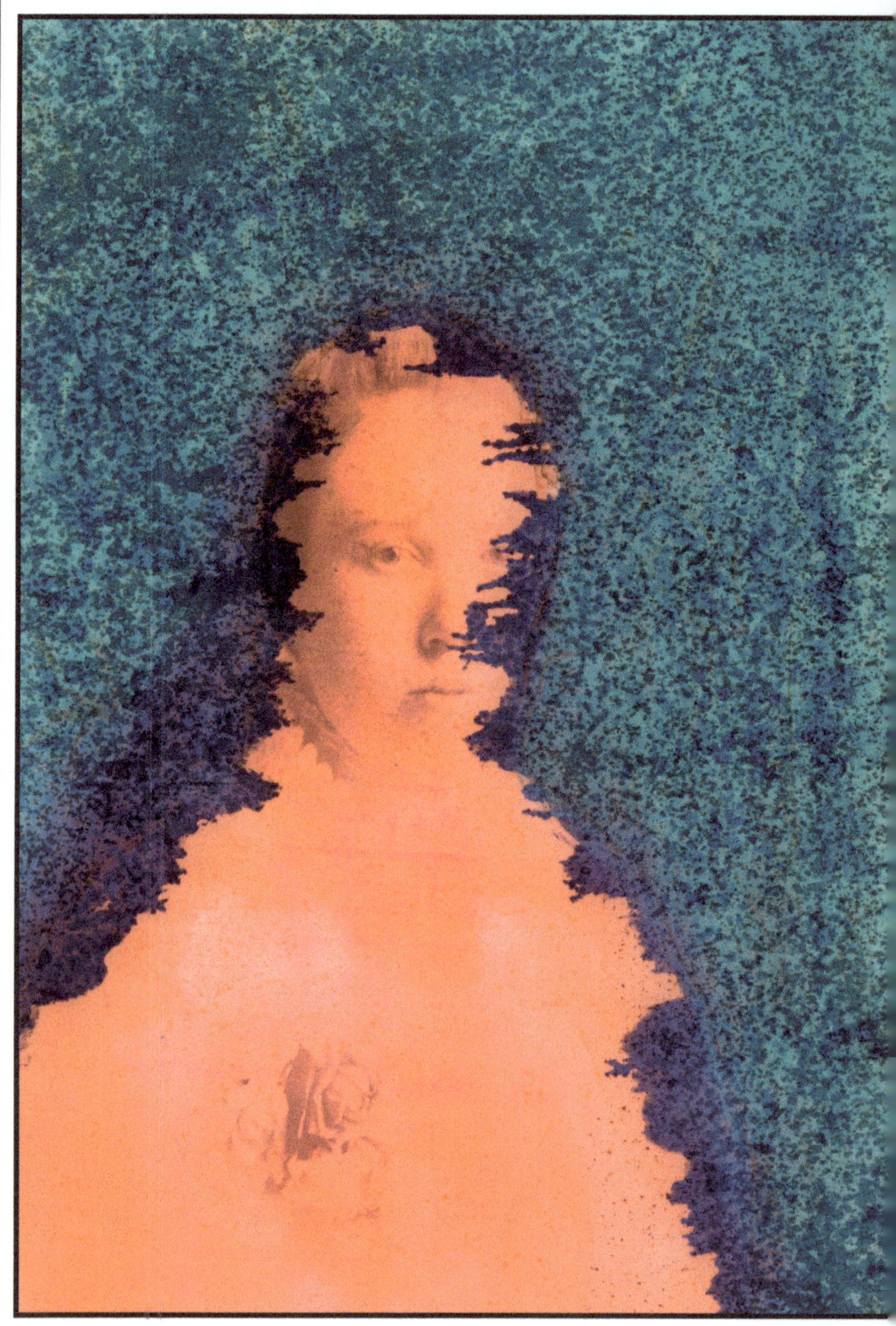

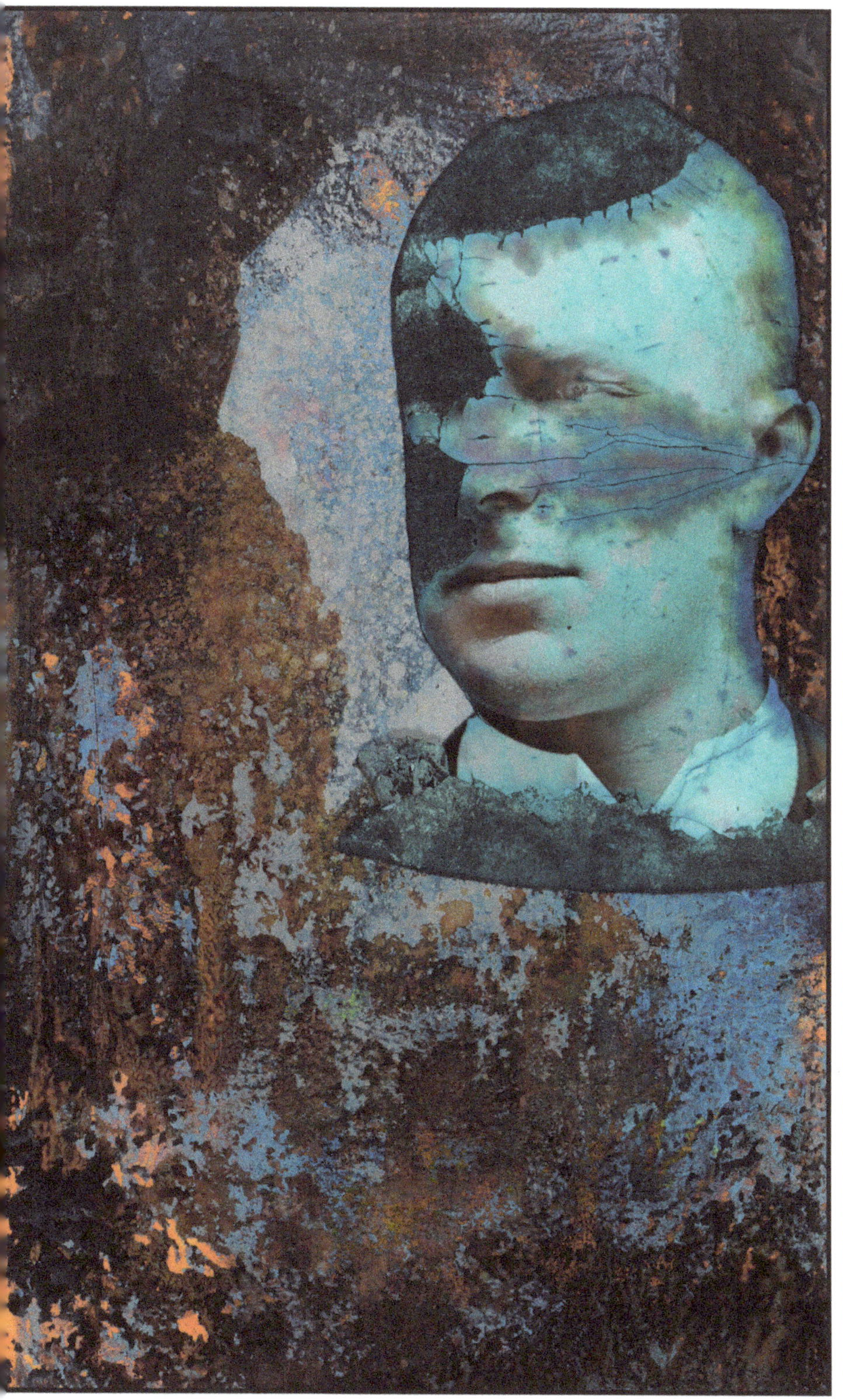

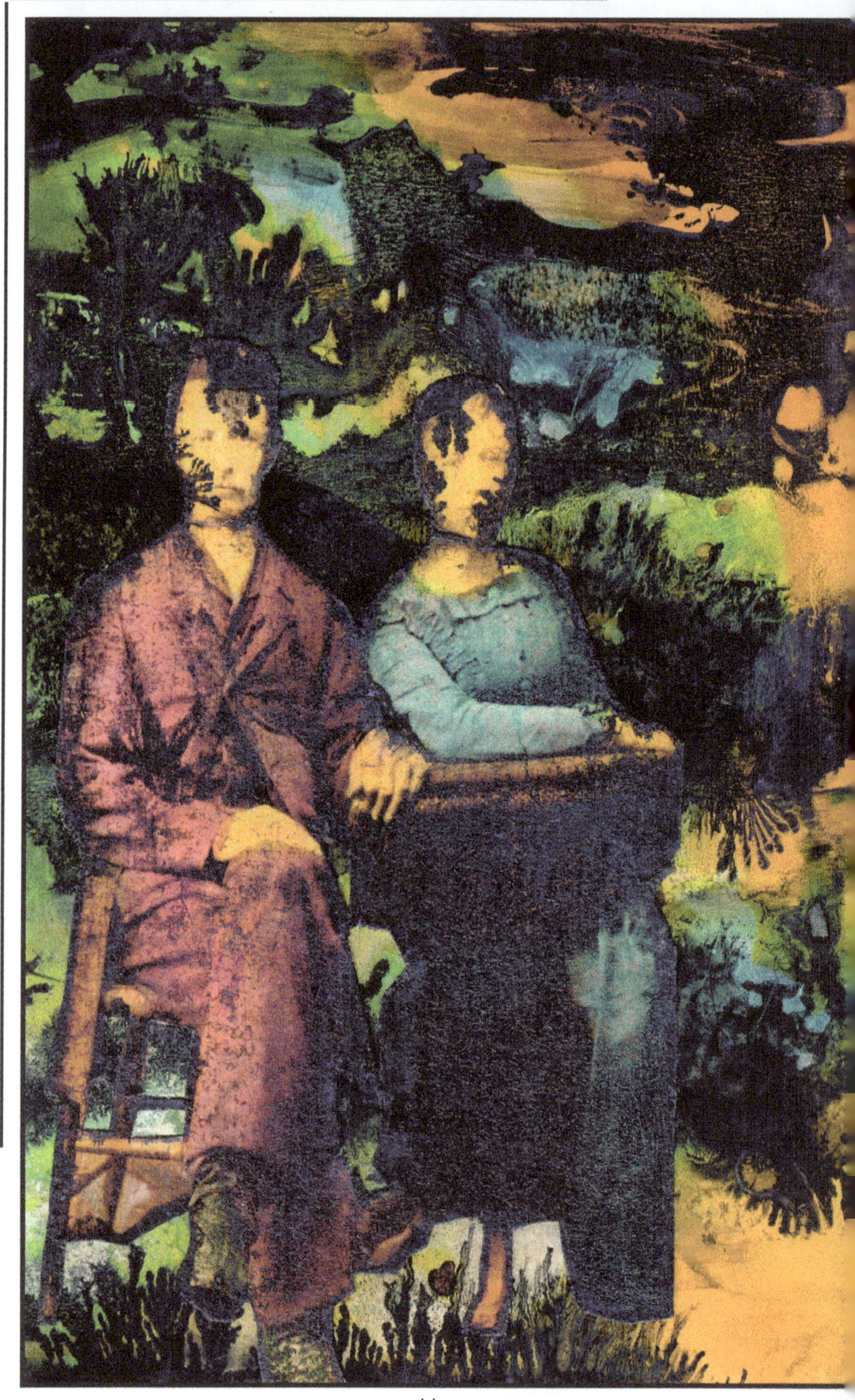

Sliced Collages

Gillian Loop

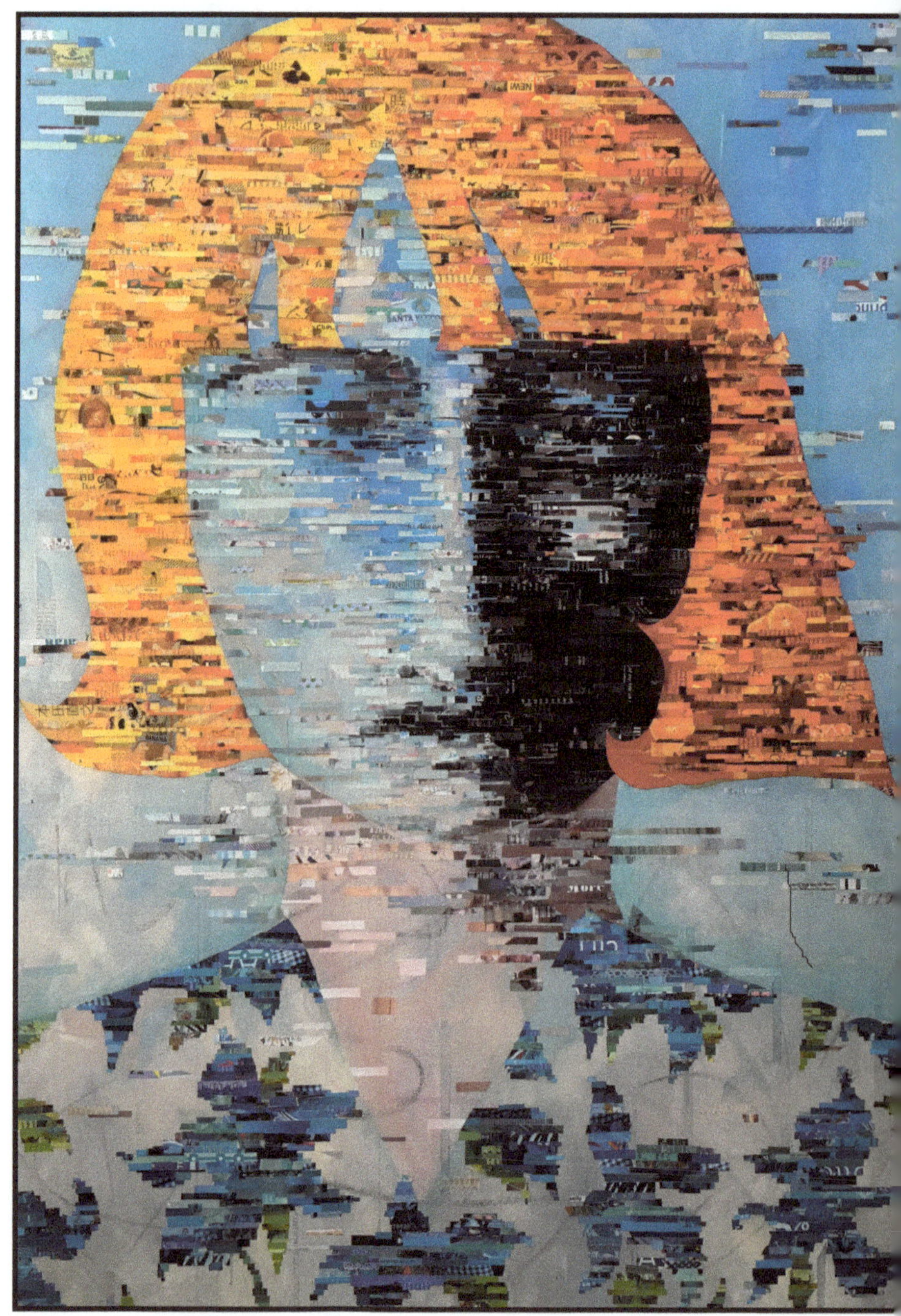

Facade

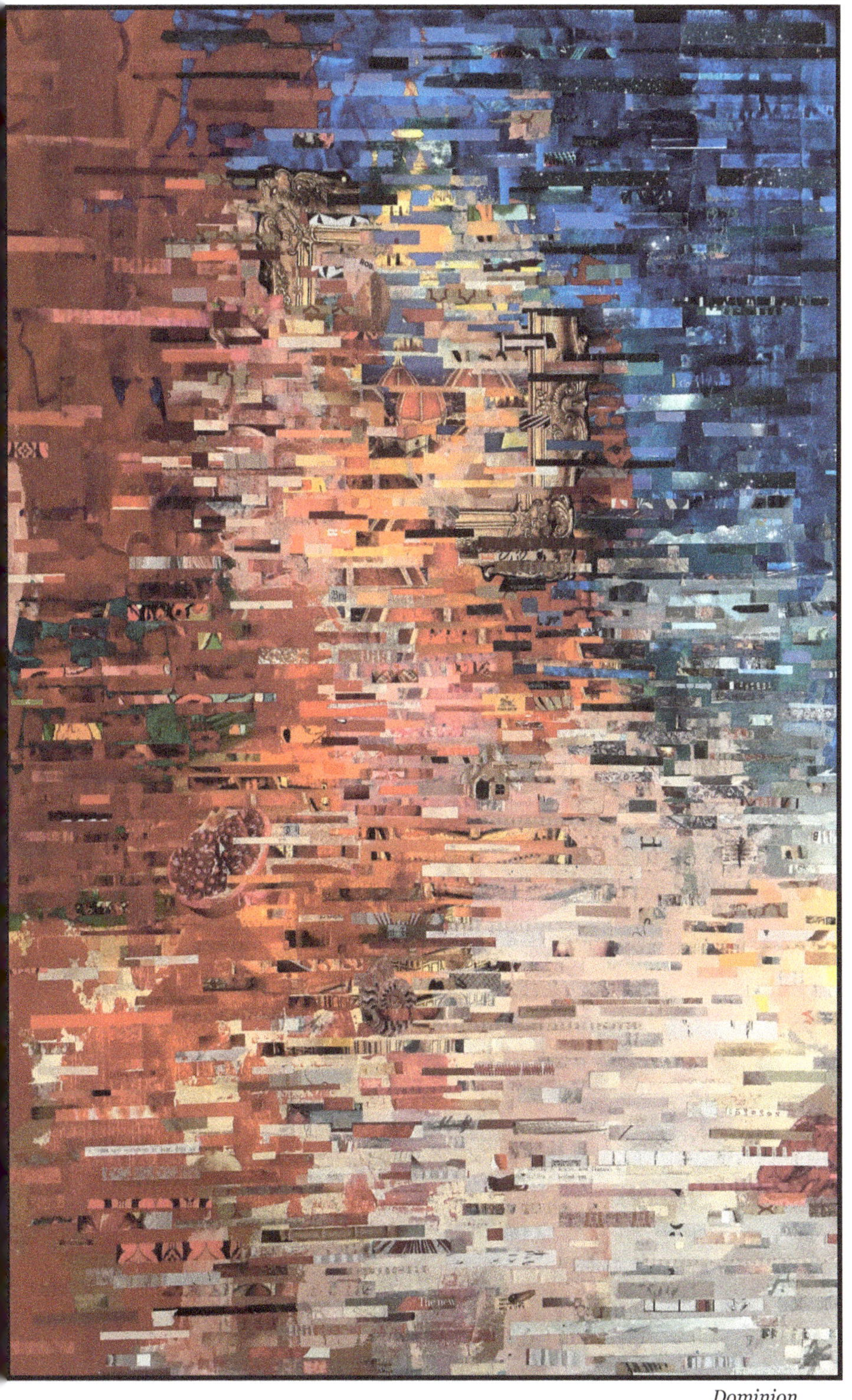

Dominion

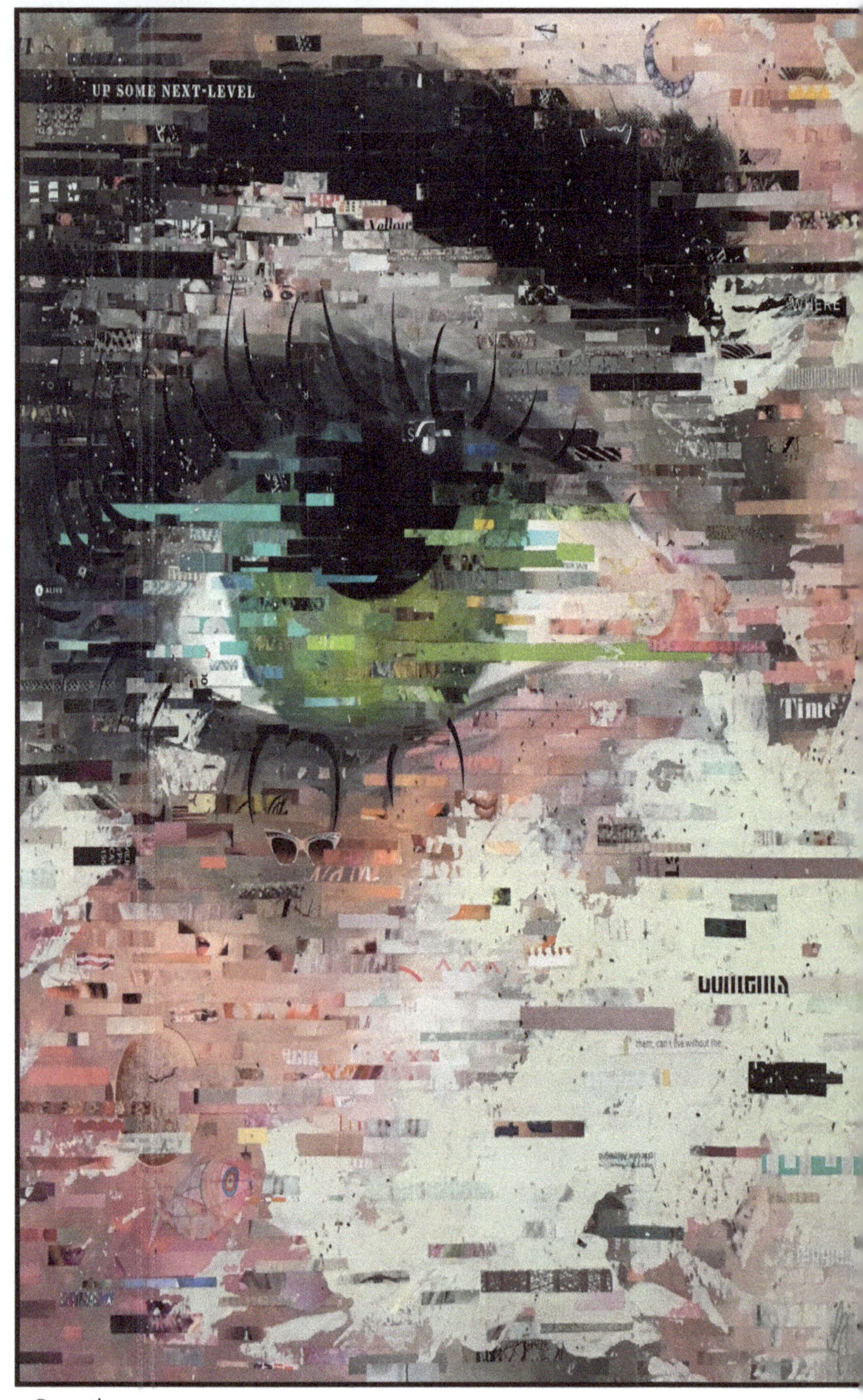

Cosmetic

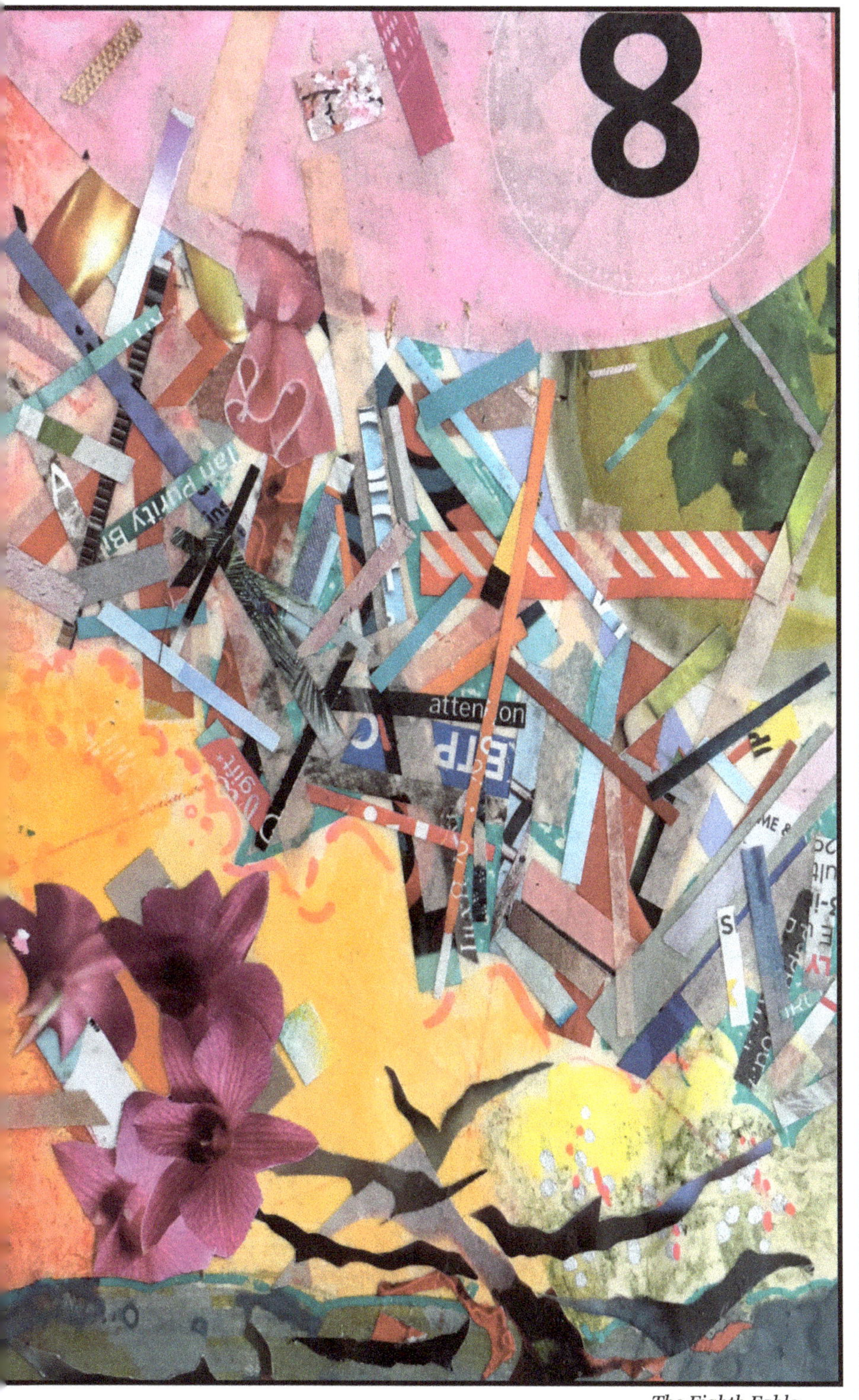

The Eighth Fable

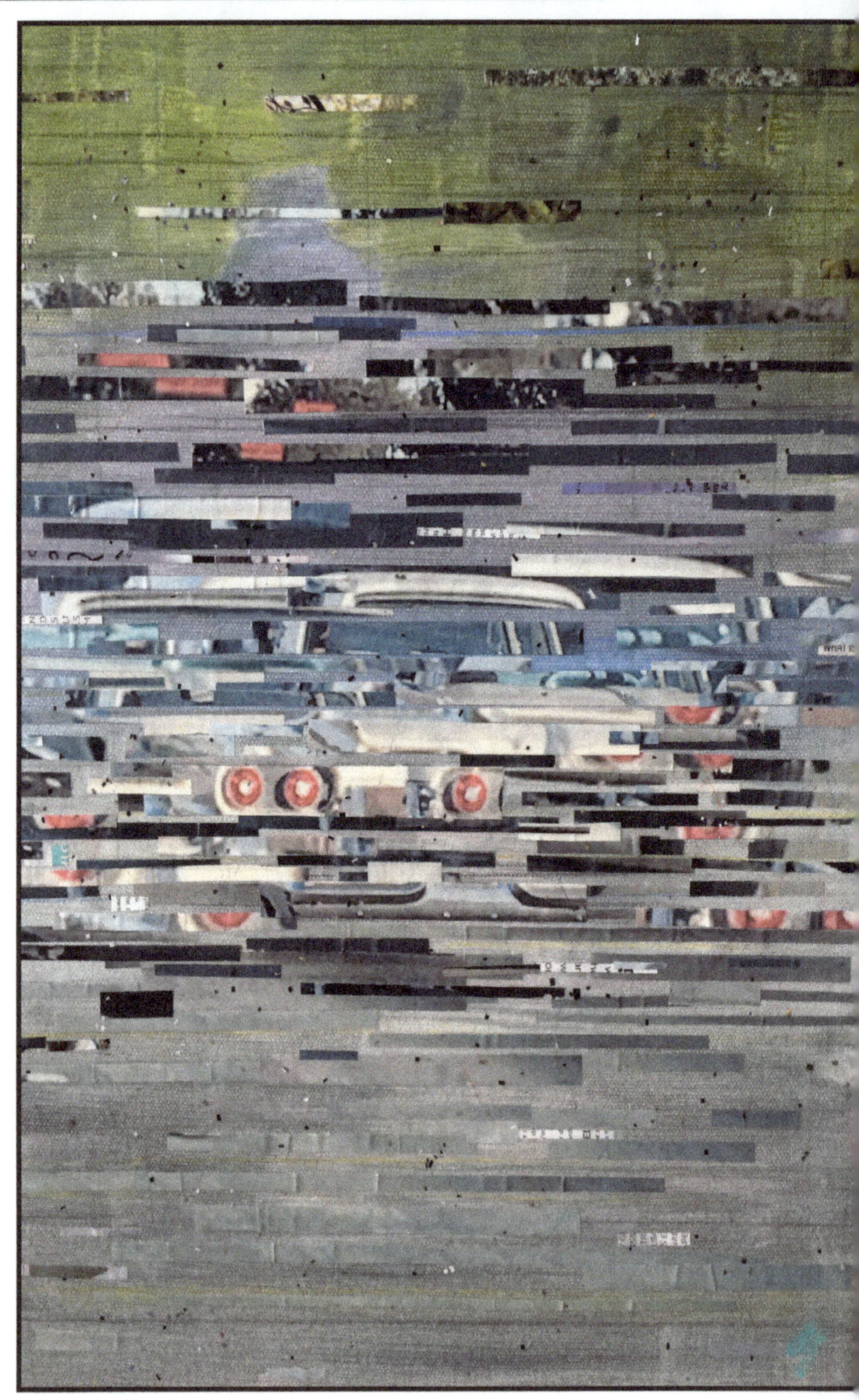

Sunday Drive

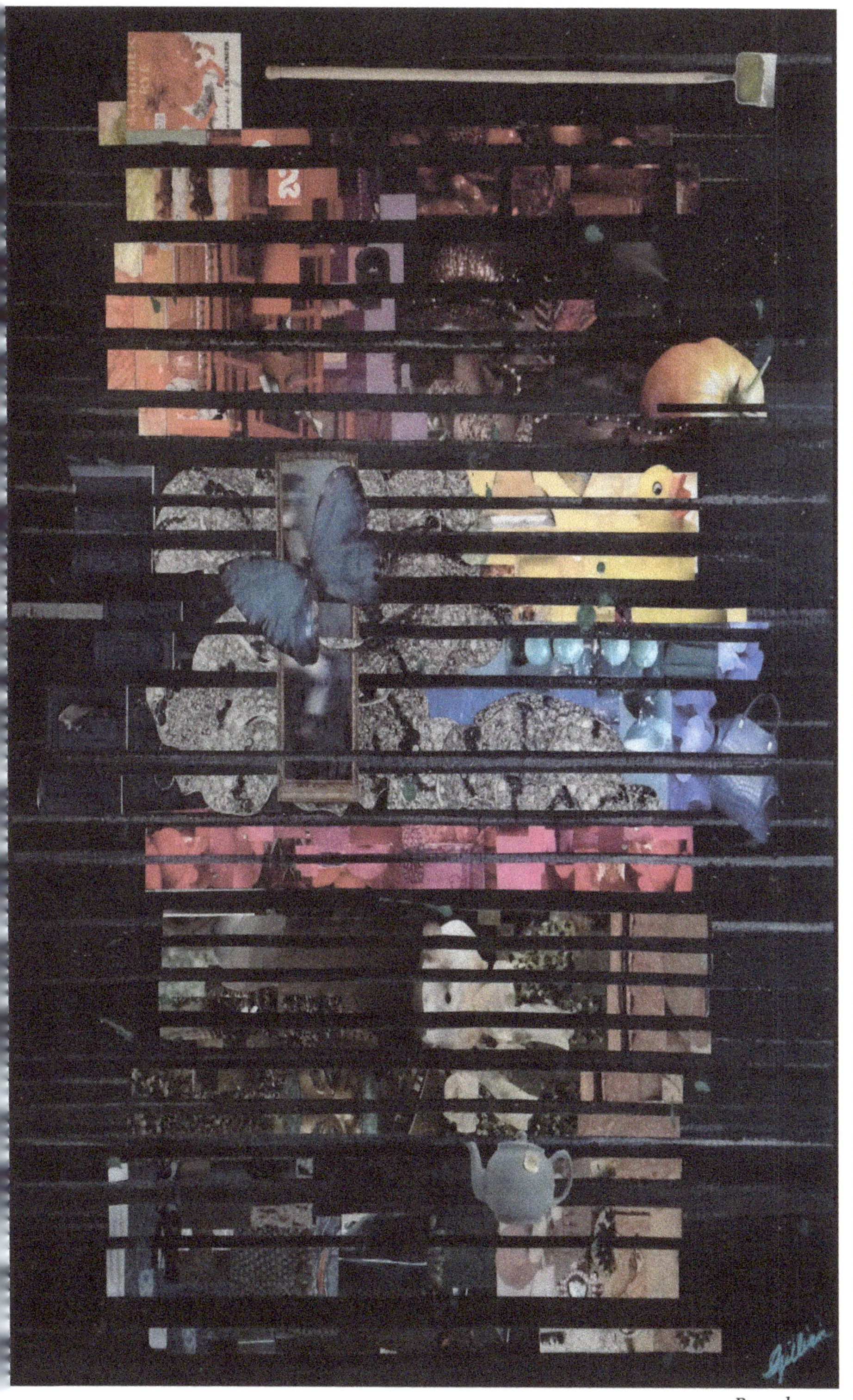

Broach

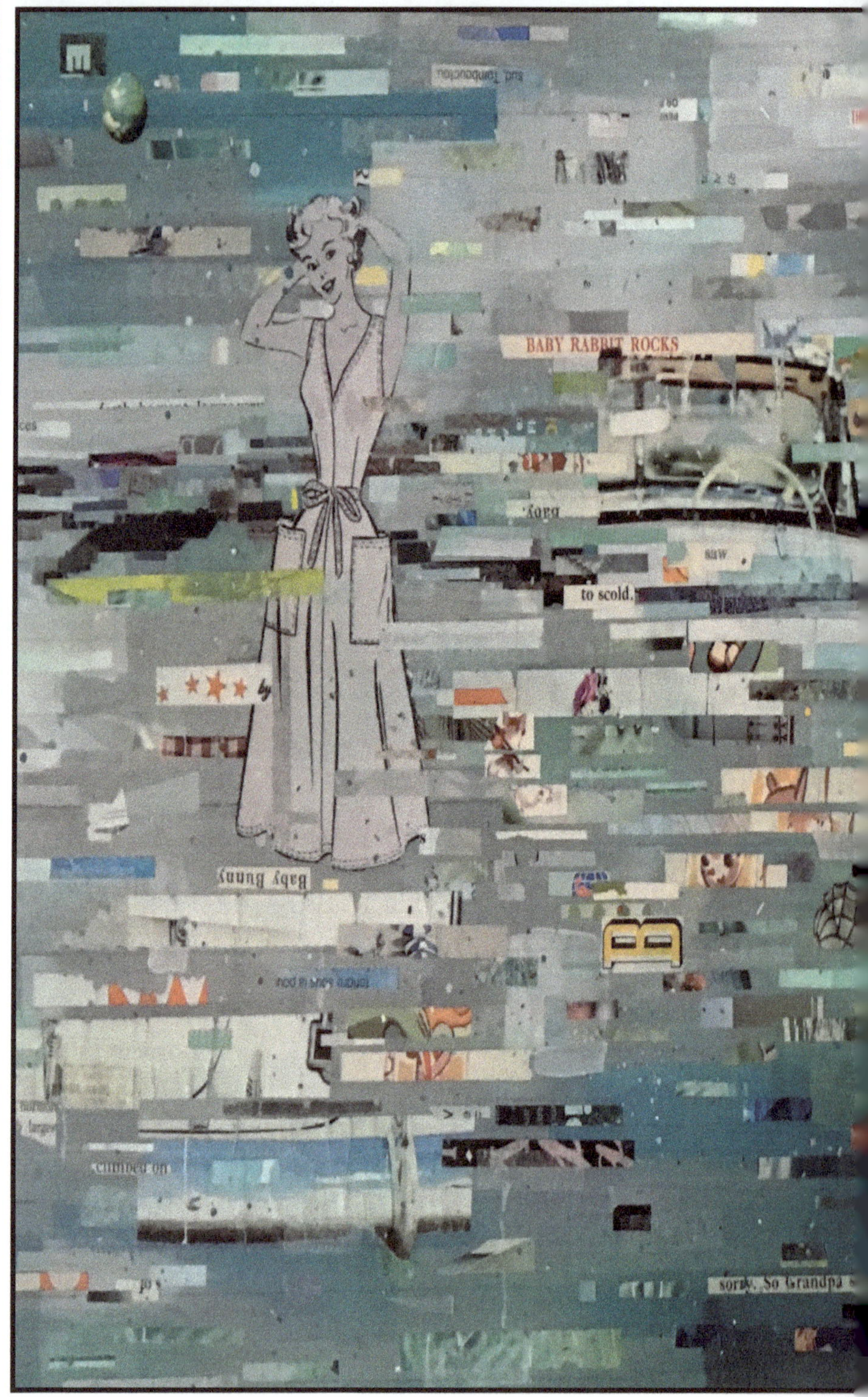

BABY RABBIT ROCKS
baby,
saw
to scold.
Baby Bunny
climbed on
sorry. So Grandpa

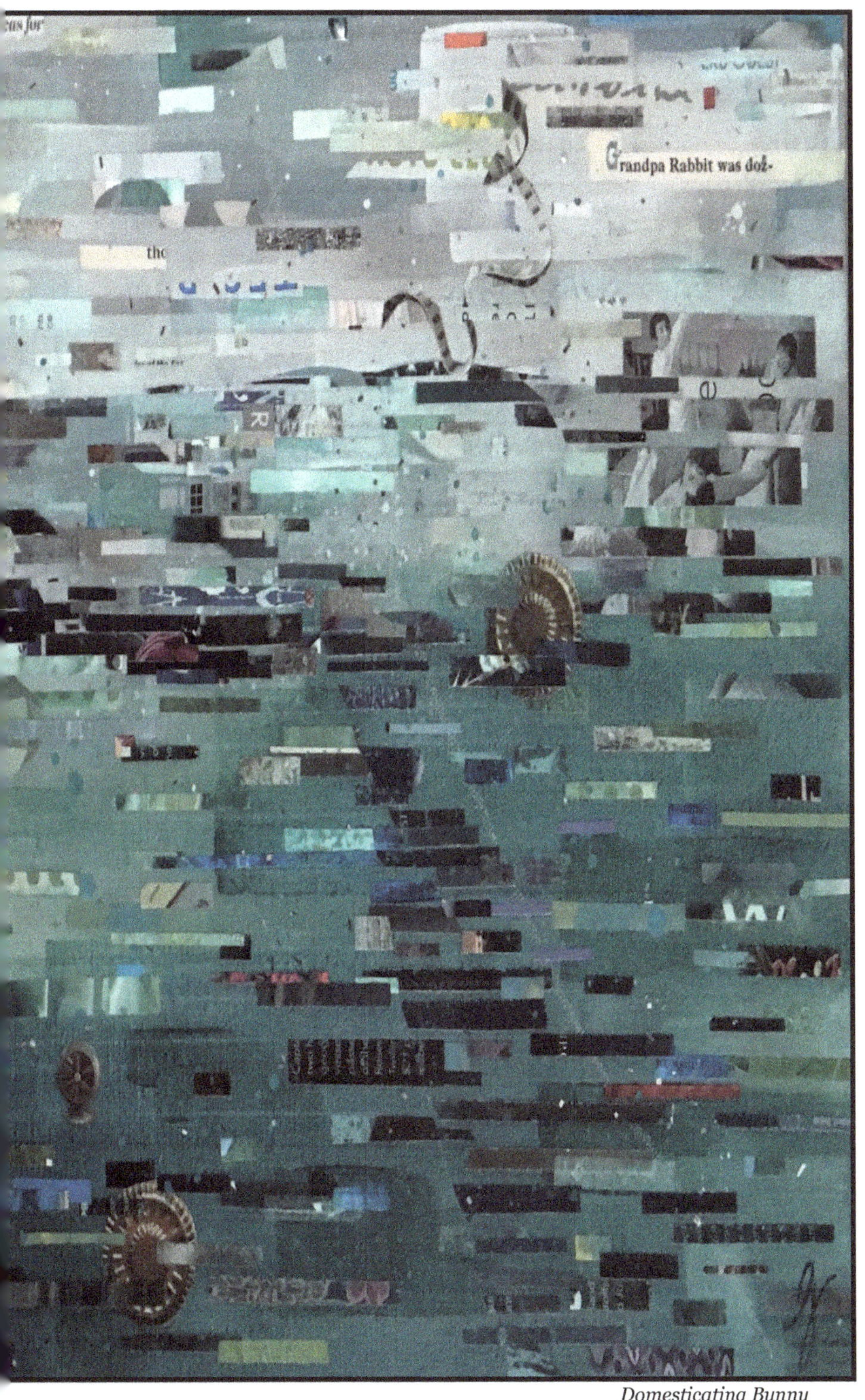

Domesticating Bunny

EPILOGUE DELIVERY

Leon Fedolfi

Mephitic feet of progress plodded up my driveway
Paused by my child's red rubber ball and
Kicked it at my small and noble dog
Proceeded up my steps
To relieve himself on my only living
Ficus Lyrata

Progress then knocked on my door
And as we came ahead, held a mirror to my face
And said, "Ok Boomer"

My fist balled in the density of a neutron star
I said in kind, "Get a job"

Ironically, I punched the mirror.

A Message to My Fellow Millennials

Paul Benkendorfer

You know, being a Millenial myself I am often reminded of just how lazy and entitled my generation is. And for good reason. We are so entitled. That's right, you heard me, entitled. Like spoiled children, all we do is complain. We demand things we have no right to. Things like affordable housing, or wages that actually compensate our labor, or (worse yet) free college tuition.

Our generation, and Gen-Z for that matter, should be grateful to have college so readily available to us. Sure, the price of college tuition has drastically increased since the 70s when our parents went. Remember, they slaved away at grueling part time jobs to pay their way. Boomers had to work an overbearing 380 hours to afford a year of college tuition. What's our generation's excuse? Oh, we have to work 3,249 hours a year on minimum wage to afford one year of college tuition in comparison? That's just us making excuses to justify our laziness. If the Boomers could do it, so can we.

And why do we act like we need college? You can just as easily go down to one of the several local factories and work just like your grandpappy did. And you have it better than he did. He worked in that factory for 16 hours a day at $5 an hour. Whereas you can earn up to $15 an hour. That's triple the pay, if you don't account for inflation! Or better yet, you can go get a trade job. Why try to follow your dreams and live the life you want? Those never work out.

I mean sure, most of those jobs have been moved overseas or have been (or will soon) be replaced by automation thus causing an entire section of society to become unemployed and unemployable, but it's how the American economy used to be. Which means it's still viable in today's global economy. It's not like we already work harder and more hours than previous generations for far less pay. All it means is that we should work more jobs and longer hours. Boomers did it.

Millennials, let's face it, getting a college degree and becoming the most educated generation in history was our biggest mistake. We chose to take on the burden of crippling debt while entering one of the worst job markets since the Great Depression. I know we were promised since we were little that college would help make our lives better, but it was our mistake for believing it.

It was our fault for taking on exorbitant amounts of debt. Not the people who raised the cost of tuition and crashed the global economy for their own selfish reasons. It was our fault. We made a dumb mistake and should have known better. It's not like these were life-altering decisions left up to people too young to legally drink or smoke.

What's most alarming is now there are those among us who have the audacity to demand free college. That's pretty outrageous for our generation to believe that higher education should be affordable to anyone. Just because the bulk of entry level jobs require a degree doesn't mean you have to go, or should go. It's not like those with college degrees end up earning more money and are less likely to be unemployed.

But if you must insist on going to college you better go into the STEM field, because virtually every other degree is worthless. Granted teachers are necessary and there are entire subsections of the economy in need of those dumb liberal arts degrees like writing and art, but those are the useless jobs. Speaking of teachers, where do they get off demanding a well funded educational system and livable wages? Come on, I don't have children, so why should I care about whether or not future generations receive a good education? It's not like their ability to contribute to the economy when they're older is going to impact me in any way. And if teachers want a livable wage they should do their job properly first.

What's next, we're going to start demanding free health care because it's not "affordable"?

Let's all take the time and remember that healthcare isn't a right. You are not entitled to seeing a doctor or preserving your own well being. Where is it written that you have the right to not die? It's your responsibility to take care of yourself, not mine or anyone else's. If you didn't want to go financially bankrupt you should have thought about that *before* you got cancer.

When it comes to health care, we should listen to our elders. Who better than the generation currently living off of Medicare, Medicaid and Social Security to lecture us on the dangers of socialized healthcare? No one, that's who.

And if that wasn't bad enough, here we go complaining about non-issues like "Climate Change." As if we have a right to unpolluted air, clean oceans, a functioning ecosystem and healthy standards of living. If sucking in coal was good enough for your great-grandfather working in the mines, it's good enough for you. Sure there is a dramatic increase in droughts and natural disasters, but those are simply natural occurrences. Nothing to be alarmed about.

So please, let's stop with this obsessive whining. All we want is free, free, free. We don't want to work for anything. Maybe if necessities such as housing, tuition and healthcare were affordable there would be no demand that they be free. It should be obvious to anyone that the people who grew up in a time without Internet, cellphones and other modern tech know better about the world than us. And it's time we listened.

English in Freefall

Jean Fineberg

Last Febuary, I was chomping at the bit to move up in the world,
so I says to my friend, "If you don't mind me asking, do you have a realitor?"
He was enamored with his, who supposably did do diligence,
so I poured over her pamplet and it peaked my interest.

I contracted her and we conversated.
Since I won't make due with just anything,
and it's my perogative, and intregal to my healthness, to live where I want,
I proscribed my principle criteria, which is a room large enough for my bed-
room suit,
and I wouldn't mind a nearby libary or expresso or sherbert shops, excetera.
I was enervated, waiting with baited breath in tenderhooks because
the idea of a sneak peak at new homes wet my appetite .

I gave her free reign, and she preceded to comprise a list,
appraising me of some track homes.
I'm not adverse to the inter city,
but I was taken back and went nuculer
when I saw drug attics wrecking havoc on the sidewalks,
a moratorium (who knows how many people are interned there)
and a crumbling ampitheater.
I started to loose my motivations
when nothing passed the mustard, and I can attest
it was a tortuous experience for the both of us.

We all ready seen allot when my inertia was
farther nipped in the butt because by in large,
her ideas were all together different than mine.
She seemed disinterested in my perspective.
For all intensive purposes, we just didn't jive.
The affect of that was us continuing to symbiote
begged the question, and became a mute point.

When I inferred that I could of honed in on simular prospects myself,
she was unphased, eluding to an admittance
that she didn't mean to flout her expertness.
However, under her self depreciating manner lurked a deep seeded intent
to extract revenge and paint me as the escape goat.
Irregardless, I use to be more sensitive, but now I'm just bemused
because if she thinks I feel badly, she has another thing coming,
and I could care less!

It's a doggy dog world, and affordable houses are first come first serve.
The media is in agreeance with the pundints
and the data says that noone can afford to live here any more.
I told that mischevious realitor (tongue and cheek)
that if worse comes to worse, I may have to take a different track,
do a 360, and become an ex-patriot.

Athenian

S Akhtar

She scents herself before she does it,
the way the powerful used to order queens to bathe in perfumes
in the bible. There was a eunuch, her favourite eunuch actually
called Haggai. They never get enough praise, though forgive her
if she gets the pronoun wrong. She never did have the right
motherly advice sisters example of turning herself in to
art, in examining the balayages or appliqués, strange
words and manners but regardless with steady hands
she lathers on scented cream and
sucks in the tumble dryer of slicked down provisions
as her hands pass over it, a dreadful harmony but sadly
better than her eyes catching a glimpse of this
overbloated extremity, like a messenger turning foot,
like a startled young soldier snapping to attention and yelling back
to the commandant stuck inside her that Sir, you are still attractive,
sir. She'd rather not, frankly.
She does the latch up first sends it over her head fully formed
like a righteous goddess or like she could be that goddess
stepping in to her right to be that goddamn goddess —
she too has a martian mercuriality
she too can rampage and stop herself
before kicking that first domino to havoc.
She passes her arms through and over wheezes and stretches
it down adjusts the belts and straps reminds herself
of the old psychiatric chairs for no reason
other than it seems relevant.
It's not. Not really.
It's over and she has admonished herself back to reality.
She can bend now without heaving ill fated
battallions together in a primordial smash.
She wears bonaparte's cap to complete the look and
until the day is gone and there is only one good reason
when this rigmarole matters in reverse:
when that latch is undone by another's hands and that artful spine
stretches up for a real and valid reason, separating pawns
reversing bishops and flinging back knights.

Taken

Amanda McNeal

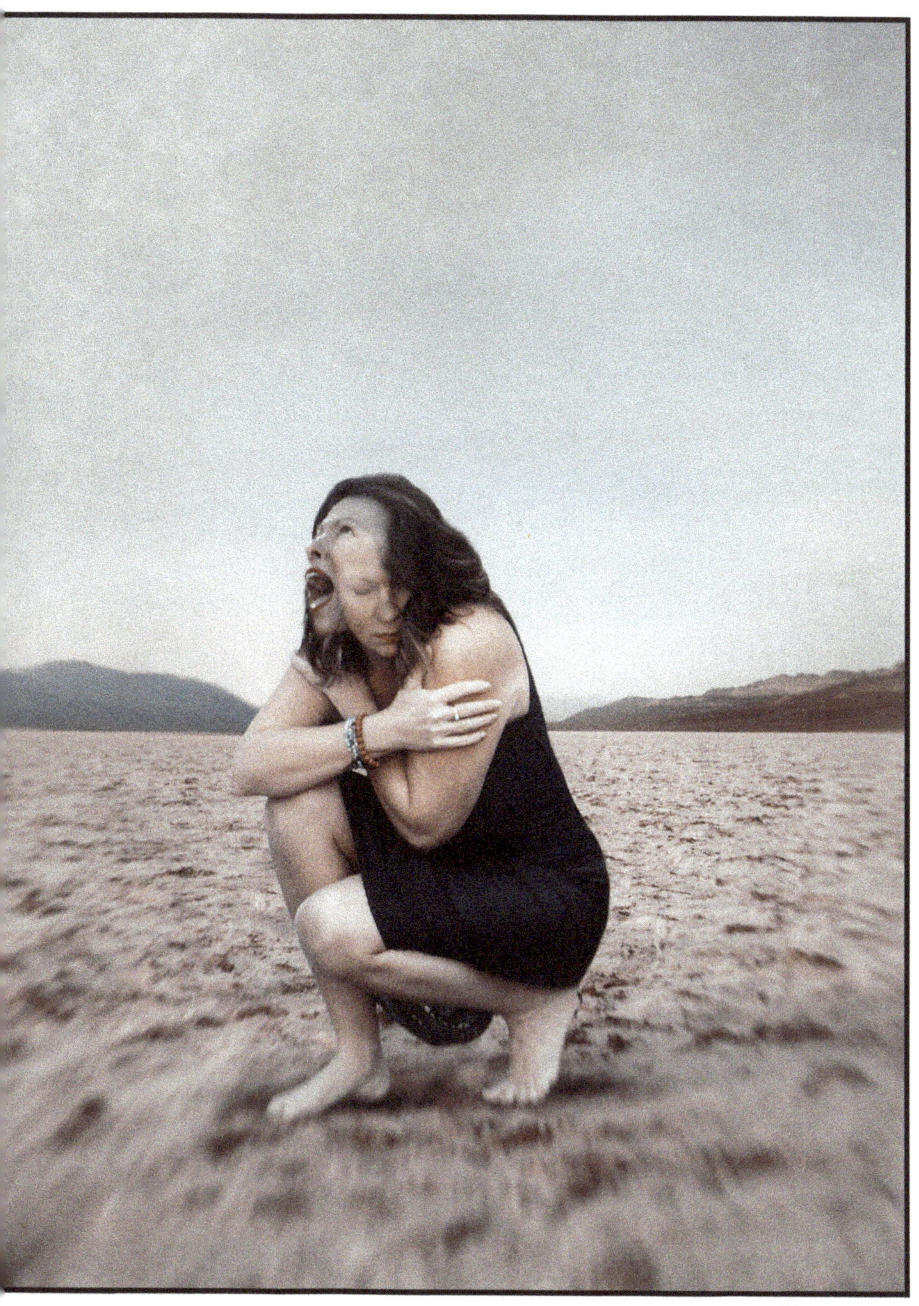

Monster

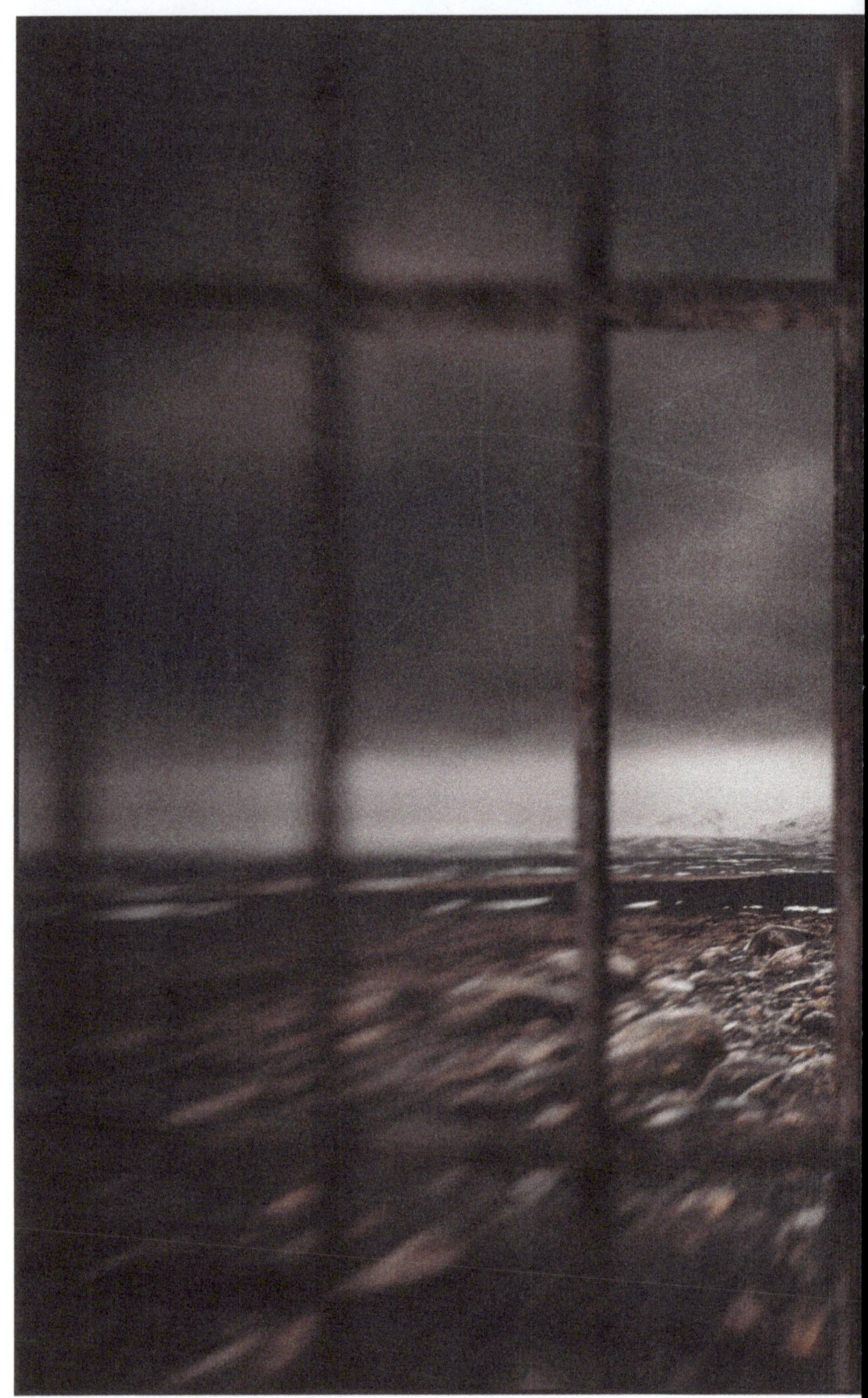

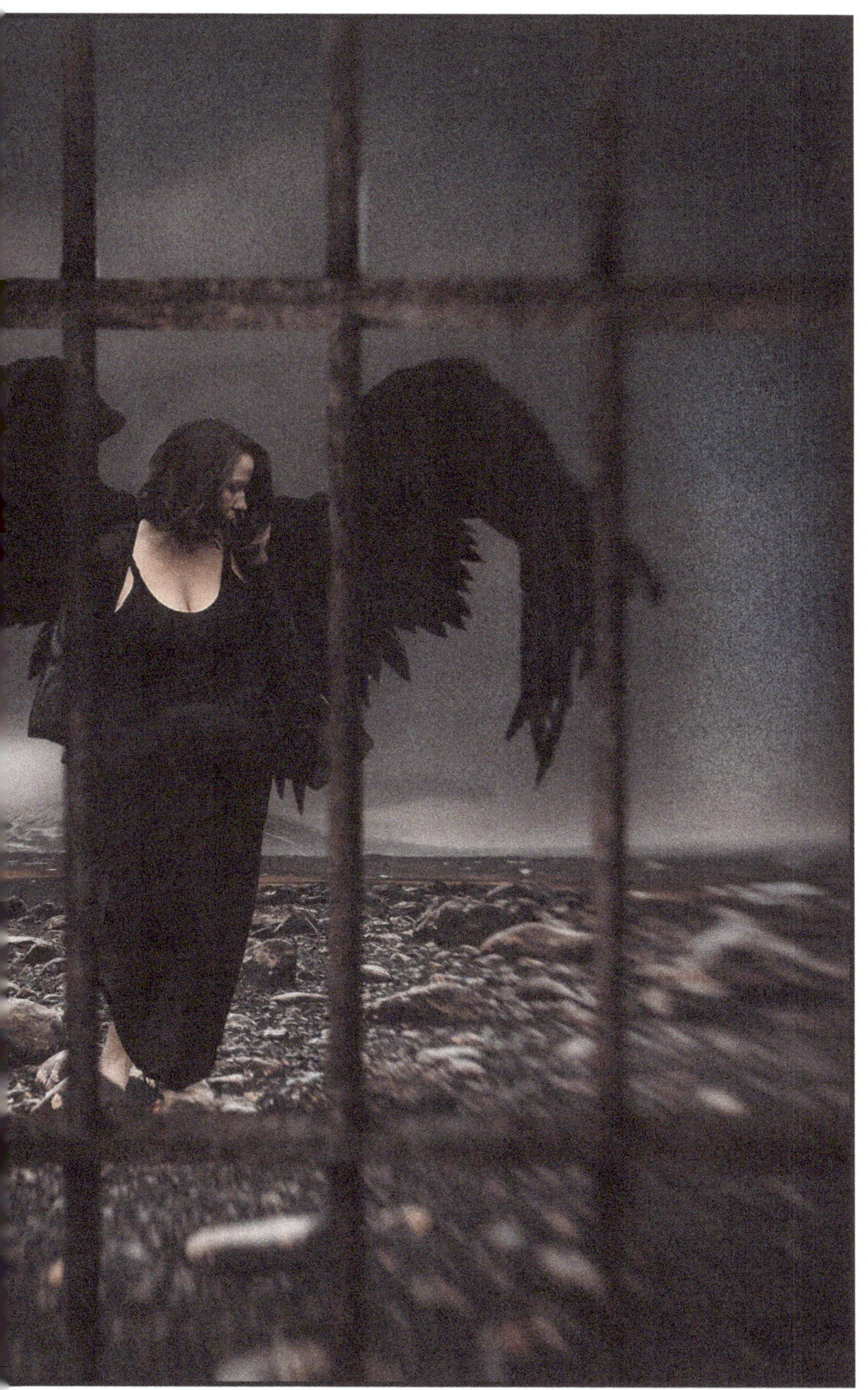

Caged

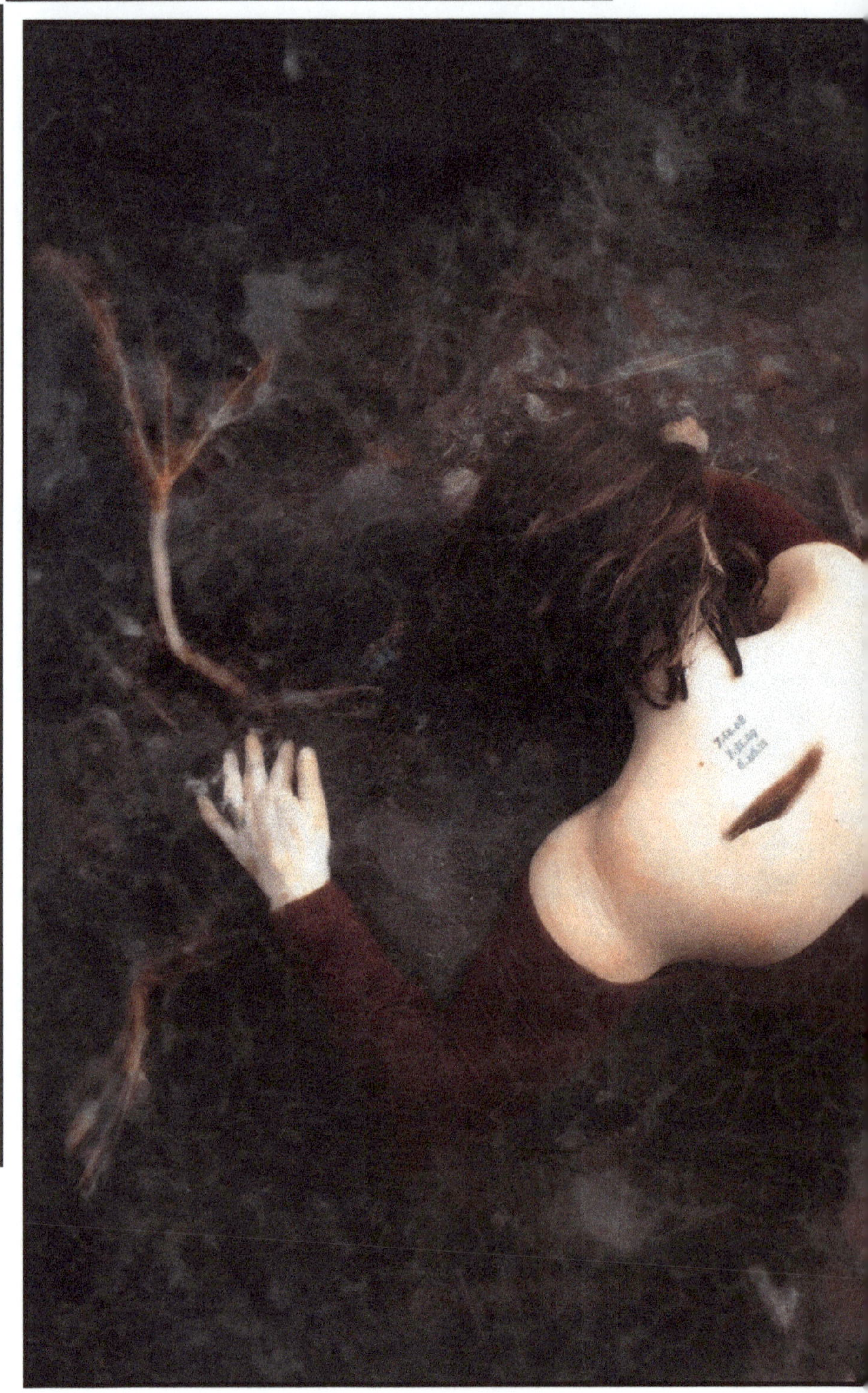

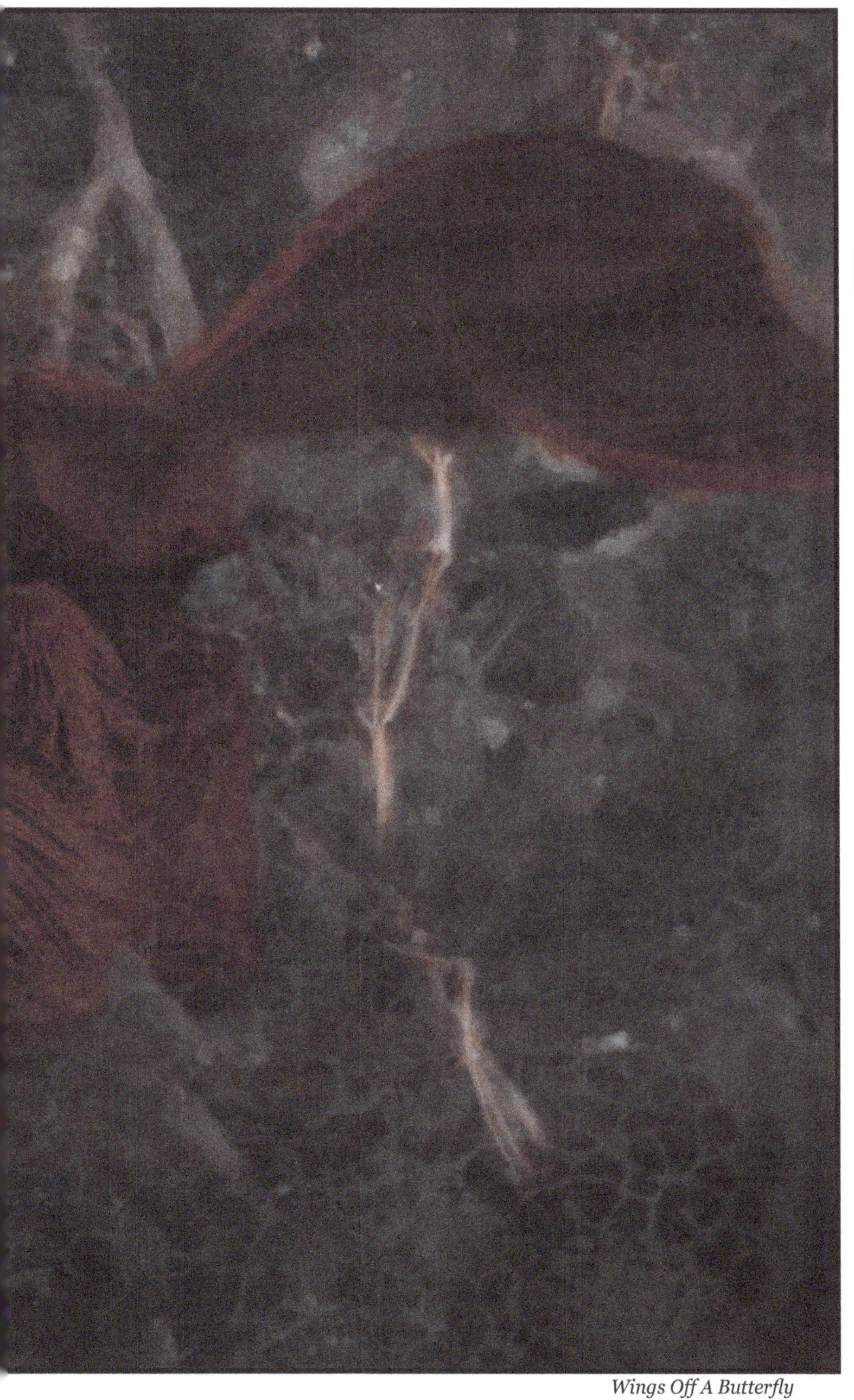

Wings Off A Butterfly

TW: Trigger Warning

Sadie Hoagland

Warning: Everything below is true.

Trigger Warning: The following piece contains content that some readers might find disturbing.

Trigger Warning: This story has some stuff about drugs in it. If you are trying to quit smoking crack, don't read the ending. If you are on meth, don't read the beginning. If you are trying to quit heroin, good fucking luck, but also don't read any of this.

T.W.: Sexual Assault.

~~Warning: This is a story with a very relatable character, exactly like you, who thinks about suicide for an entire day. It's just, like, a really bad day. If you have suicidal thoughts today, don't read this story. Or maybe it's exactly what you need. But we can't take that risk.~~

Trigger Warning: The author of this piece has been mildly sexually assaulted on the street, on the metro. Men have attempted to coerce her, emotionally and physically manipulate her. Men have commented on her appearance and her body and made sexual innuendos in a professional setting. She has been clinically depressed for periods of her life, and has had suicidal thoughts. She was stalked in college, and all her friends treated it like an ongoing joke. She, like many women, has a story where later she asked herself, her best friend, was that rape?

Warning: This story contains a heartbreaking scene in which a woman breastfeeds a starving old man during the depression. If you've experienced extreme poverty, or hunger, or Steinbeck, this story may trigger traumatic episodes.

Trigger Warning: The following piece contains content that some readers might find disturbing. More specifically, this story contains a rape scene. My characters and setting and description are rendered so vividly that if you read this, you will undoubtedly feel like you are there, in the moment. You might not be able to handle this.

Warning: This story contains a scene where the character is told to get over "it." It being the worse you can imagine. It being pretty bad. It being a passing comment a colleague makes about her ass. It being ambiguous.

Trigger Warning: The author's stalker—after three years, her friends joking the whole time—well, he went for her. She told him to get out. He punched her on the jaw. She didn't tell her friends, because, well, she was already the punchline. Ha ha, she thought, rubbing the knobbed bone below her ear.

Warning: This story contains death, overt misogyny, imperialistic flexings, and the weather on Kilimanjaro.

Trigger Warning: This story contains rough sex between a man and a woman that may or may not be consensual. For the female character she is unsure, even it as is happening, if she wants this. If you are reader who has experienced this, you might want to skip pages 2-9. The male character does think it is consensual, but if you are a male reader who has ever vaguely wondered if the sex you are having is in fact consensual, you might want to avoid the story all together. Am I right?

Trigger Warning: When one assault happened, the author didn't know who to tell. She had told an older woman about the one where the man grabbed her breast violently on the street. The older woman told she should rethink her wardrobe. She looked down at her jean skirt and wanted to feel deep shame but instead felt ambivalence. And then a second woman shamed the older woman who had said that about the wardrobe to the point of tears. The author ended up comforting the woman who had blamed the whole thing on her skirt and was now crying. And she kept wearing that skirt. She read books all summer in that skirt.

Warning: This story contains a character who reads a story with no trigger warning. The character feels something.

T.W. Train Accident

Warning: This story contains a woman who practices necrophilia over the course of several years. The whole town finds out at the end. The reveal is subtle and there are not any gruesome details, but the feeling is unsettling so as a reader you might want to avoid this.

Warning: This story contains intrigue beyond measure.

Trigger Warning: This story might need a trigger warning because they seem popular and I don't want anyone to effing freak out and end up having a breakdown or whatever so I'm just playing it safe. Here's all the stuff in my story that might disturb someone: A child smoking. A child drinking. A child finding a dildo, and unsure what it is, using It to play tug of war with the dog. So maybe animal abuse, too. A woman looking into a mirror. A man leaving his fly unzipped. A child breaking a coffee mug and cutting herself. But by accident. But it's in there and there's lots and lots of blood.

Trigger Warning: Most often, the author told no one. Or a close friend. And then moved on. Became an academic. She was lucky nothing happened that kept her from moving on, though some things were harder than others. Also here's the thing: you knew it happened to everyone. So why tell them? Or because you might be shamed. Or you might ruin the joke. Or they'd know you can't take a joke.

Can't you take a joke?

Warning: This story contains literal triggers! Lots of guns. Not as many as the news, but still. There are several mass shootings and NRA protesters and even several experimental scenes that document the minutiae of gun legislation debates in several states.

Warning: This story contains multi-generational, pathological racism. This story contains a lynching. This story contains no saving grace. Because it's about a fucking lynching.

Warning: This story contains animal abuse. We can all agree animal abuse is horrible. But not as bad as child abuse? Or is it? It's not an easy thing to read or think about, certainly. But unless you are an animal, specifically a pug, that has been abused, this really shouldn't be a "trigger" for you. If you are a pug that has been abused and your owner, in an act of further abuse, reads this story aloud to you, I am sorry, I truly am.

The author is older now, and sometimes young women tell her about things that have happened to them. Some things are bad, and there are times when she wishes she could do more. That she commanded a militia of vigilante justice. Or had a bat phone, in world where Batman was a feminist. Because it turns out Title IX is pretty useless.

Warning: This story contains all sorts of shit I stole from peoples' Facebook feeds. It's problematic, but they didn't have trigger warnings on facebook but now that I've made them literature, which is something else, they require a trigger warning.

Warning: This story contains multiple characters talking about a war. What has happened, who died and how, etc. It's pretty fucking devastating. Be warned. But you have to read it for your assignment.

Warning: I wrote this story because our teachers said "write your fears" and my worst fear, besides being mauled to death by a bear, is losing my girlfriend in some kind of accident. Seriously I got so sad while I was writing this. If something like this has happened to you, I can't tell you how sorry I am and I really am because even just imagining it left me sobbing. And like I can't even tell her that, because it would be too weird, you know? So she just thinks I'm extra clingy this week because I can't say to her: I wrote this story and really had to think about how much you mean to me and how my life is better with you because I like really, really thought about your death. I can't say that, can I?

Sometimes the author feels like a passive receptacle for these stories about creepy men. Sometimes men she knows. A vessel. How Freudian.

T.W. Supreme Court Justice Confirmed

Warning: This story contains references to the evils that men do. By men, I mean mankind. So, women, too. The evils that men and women and other nonbinary genders, inclusively, do.

Warning: This essay is about the time I tried to kill myself. It was fucking horrible time in my life and really hard to write about. But I didn't have a trigger warning for writing the story, I just had to think about that time over and over again and now you have to read about it. But I wanted to write it. I needed to write it. But you don't have to read it. This warning is me, saying, even though I struggled then and struggled again to write this, you don't have to read it.

You have an out. You get to turn away from me right now, in this moment, if that is what you want. If your own shit is just too much for you to see that other people are having an experience. That other people might be able to understand you. That other people might know. You.

Sometimes when a young woman complains about something stupid a man has said, the author, she is ashamed to admit, thinks big deal. Or, Wow, a man said something stupid? A man? Shocking. She is, behind those words, thinking of all the things much worse that have happened to her. She is outwardly sympathetic, as that is required. She doesn't want to be shamed, or shame anyone. But inside she's tough as nails and wants these women to be too, because if they let these comments derail them, then what?

Warning: This story contains abortion. This is a sensitive topic, but in my story it's very simple. The character is a skinny teenager raped by her elderly father nightly and he also sodomizes her daily with a beer bottle. She becomes pregnant. That's pretty much it.

Sometimes young women also tell her they are aware of the emotional workload that women in her position bare. But still they needed to talk. They needed to feel seen. I am sorry you are the vessel, but look, you are the vessel, they say.

Warning: The story is about bigots. At times the bigots, before they are mowed down by our heroes, use the kind of language bigots would use. I've bleeped the words out, but you will be able to guess what they are and if the guessing makes you uncomfortable, you might not want to read it.

The author would never dream of talking or writing about her own experiences, herself. But she does get a secret pleasure out of writing trigger warnings for can-onized literature.

Trigger Warning: My life has sometimes been difficult, so to write it for you might cause you trauma beyond measure. I mean you got upset about the phrase "stay-at-home mom" in my last story, so I'm guessing you can't handle my childhood.

Because mostly she'd assumed it would be boring to others.

Warning: This story is about you. And the time you. And the way you felt. And you might feel that again. And that's some very scary shit. And PTSD is very real.

Or perhaps crushing. These people who tell her in tears about a way in which someone disappointed them, to hear what "adulting" was to her, it might be too much for them, too much when the end inside her that has been sharpened to a point is revealed.

Trigger warning: So as a solution, I've elected not to write it. I won't write any of these stories.

T.W.: Everything above is true.

So she elected not to write it, to try to reframe and update her mentality, to "get on board," to stitch her anger into something else. A knit vessel maybe. A red phone.

Trigger Warning: Everything above is true, and there is no story.

Trigger Warning: There is no story. I'm all ears.

Hoes Anonymous

Andrea Jefferson

For you.

On May 16, 2020, Krestin Carlisle interviews writer and entrepreneur Lavenia Hibley live over Instagram from their homes during Covid-19 quarantine.

"So what everyone's dying to know is what birthed this concept. I mean, what makes you think of something like this?"

"Really, it was simple–"

"Let's start off with who you are for our viewers at home that may just be tuning in. This is Dr. Lavenia–"

"No, no. I'm not a doctor."

"I'm sorry, I'm sorry."

"It's fine, it's fine. People assume, but no, my schooling stopped at community college. I'm educated by experience and reading pretty much now."

Awkward pause from Krestin.

"Right. Of course. Well this is Lavenia Hibley. For those of you at home, she's a blogger and is the owner and operator of Hoes Anonymous, which is very pro-woman and has been making a buzz."

Krestin smiles directly at her phone camera and into the faces of 3,400 people quarantined and curious. Comments range from "WE MISSED YOU KRESTIN" to "Whooo?" and extend themselves flavorlessly among the heap of "look at the tits on these bitches."

"Now, as you know, Lavenia, me and my supporters are all here for the feminism, and your message. Tell us a little bit about Hoes–"

Krestin gets choked up laughing and must sip from Fiji water before returning her flush-faced charisma to her audience now surpassing 5,000 viewers.

"Sorry. The title of that is just too cute to me. Tell us about Hoes Anonymous."

"It was simple. I wanted people, mainly women....and of course other sexually oppressed groups, but mainly women, uh minority women, to have a place where they could confide their sexual insecurities, interests, or even encounters they've already had. We also interact with a lot of different suicide prevention groups, and we aim to make it clear sexual crimes or revenge porn, things of that nature are never worth ending your life for. I feel especially now that we're at a time where these things are given more public aggression–"

Krestin's terrier makes himself visible to the 10.5k viewers, doubling the amount of "heart" reactions and with an exaggerated push of her foot, he is back out of frame.

"Now let me stop you there because I feel that my fans already may have a similar question as me. Are you only focused on minority women because you're a minority woman or I mean, what is it that makes sexual crimes different for you all than it does say...me?"

"No, don't get me wrong. My only focus is not minority women; please don't mistake that."

12.3k viewers' comments range from "No surprise. Give a successful Black woman a platform and the first thing she does is boohoo about color. #OverIt" to "White women no longer get assaulted? #MeToo survivor here. No one gave my rapist a memo."

"I don't at all want that to be the impression I'm giving here. I'm just saying I think White people, White women in particular, undoubtedly get a longer leash for sexual exploration than women of color, ya know?"

"I have to disagree."

"You disagree?"

Krestin nods enthusiastically.

"I *have* to disagree. I'm almost *obligated* to disagree. And the reason I say that is because I remember telling one of my close friends about this really intense one-night stand I had, and don't get me wrong she meant well. I just felt a lot of judgment from her: she was asking me questions that you're, ya know, not going to be able to answer about a one-nighter like what his name was," *Krestin giggles.*

Lavenia considers this, then nods slowly.

"It's often in our safe spaces that we're really, really tested or even exploited by people we love, and I'm sorry that happened to you. Again, Hoes Anonymous would be a service to someone like you that maybe wants to get things off her chest-"

"But how would I know that if it's targeted to minority women? I mean if something is going to be all-inclusive, it literally has to include everyone. That lack of diversity could turn away a lot of people potentially needing help and assuming it's unavailable to them."

There is a long pause from both women. 16k people have the hammers to accompany Krestin's nails; they listen hungrily for evidence Lavenia's snug in her coffin.

"It *is* diverse, but if we're being honest, the people that do benefit the most from this program are people of color. There's an anonymous entrance survey that, of course, is not a sure way of gauging the data, but it gives us a ballpark. We've gathered Black women between the ages of 15 and 33 account for the majority of our clients."

"Okay, well before we get into statistics, for our people just tuning in this is Lavenia Hibley, founder of Hoes Anonymous, which we initially viewed as a call center for all women to safely discuss consensual sexual exploits or non-consensual attacks, the like. We're learning, however, that may not be the case. Lavenia, please continue."

"I'm sorry, what are you saying? That is the case; it's not even just for women. It's *mainly* for women-"

"We don't have much time, so, Lavenia, you don't have to keep rectifying your statements. We're just here to listen."

Lavenia bites her lip as 20k people watch her from their toilet seats, lawns, kitchens. With a sigh, she offers the following:

"What's your idea of fair diversity, Krestin? Can I get a specific example?"

"Sure." *There's a pause.* "Well 'Jake From Statefarm', which is a very recognizable name for anyone not living under a rock; he's an African-American now. The original face was not. I think that's nice."

"Right, but that doesn't empower me. I never cared what race Jake From Statefarm is. I care that my cousin is a felon and therefore is legally barred from most jobs, so prior to working for Hoes Anonymous, which pays $5 above minimum wage in my state, she couldn't even afford insurance. Because Black and brown people are disproportionately affected by the prison system, this leads me to believe most are in the same boat as her. Truthfully, the majority of my staff is comprised of women with nonviolent felonies and priors-"

"So why not hire educated Black women for those positions? Wouldn't that be a better way to pay it forward to those that overcame their circumstances and put in the work to be better people?"

"Why don't you?"

"Excuse me?"

"Why aren't there more educated Black women on your staff?"

"I hire the candidates I feel are best suited for the job because unlike you, Lavenia, I don't have an agenda."

"Excuse me-"

Carlisle picks up her phone and removes Hibley from the Live.

"I'm sorry, you guys, but I couldn't handle that," *she asserts.*

Lavenia begins her own Live after being abruptly removed from Carlisle's and having both her attempts to reconnect ignored. Because she has a different audience on her own personal profile, a very meager number, if any, of the viewers on Krestin's Live get to hear Lavenia's uninterrupted point of view.

***

As the weeks pass, her business suffers from awful reviews, many of which just regard her as racist and claim Hoes Anonymous is no help to the community. The people leaving these reviews have never utilized the service.

***

Hoes Anonymous shuts its doors due to less funding and public support after a year of bad publicity. Most of the people using the service could not publicly vouch for it safely outside the avis of their social profiles.

The same year the program that gave thousands of marginalized humans a voice shuts its doors, Carlisle is named as a nominee for the National Media Award for producing a week-long special on her website showcasing WOC entrepreneurs.

Lavenia sees the award announcement from her cracked phone screen while passing a mural of Destiny Harrison, a Black woman that was fatally shot in her own hair salon before her daughter's very eyes. Lavenia locks her screen and holds her head high against the light, guarded by Destiny.

SHAME PARADE

Laurie Rosenwald

I don't want to tell a story about breaking the rules. I want to break them right now, live.

I LOVE to say things that get me into trouble like, "what's so special about half the human race?"

But Trouble is my middle name. Laurie Trouble Rosenwald. I lied. It's "Frank," a man's name. Because I've been a woman and I've been a man, and baby, let me tell you, it's a tough call, irrespective of gender. I just lied again! I've been a woman all my life. Except for the first part, when I was mostly a girl. The point is, I cannot be trusted. Women lie. We also cheat and steal. I like to steal fancy makeup. It's fun to get away with things, whether it's a $58 "Vermillion-aire" lipstick, or manslaughter.

Also, we want to let our testicles breathe on the F train, wear sunglasses on Tinder, and pee all over the toilet seat without fear of recrimination. Am I right?

Before, you could just be a man or a woman, but now you can be both, either or neither. This has nothing to do with sexual orientation. We now know that there are, in fact, three sexual orientations: straight, gay, and British. Also, "orientation" is no longer a word. Say "Asian." Arigato.

Trust me- Women aren't so great, and I've known quite a few. We're devious, disingenuous, secretive, duplicitous, unscrupulous, and make profligate, pro-miscuous use of thesaurus.com.

I'll bet you didn't know about the secret toilet cartel that meets in the ladies' rooms of selected Foot Locker locations. Topic A is YOU and your gruesome anatomical deformity.

You thought Putin was behind the 2016 Election? Nope. It was me, Amy Poe-hler and Tina Fey in the UCB Improv bathroom. Because... we just couldn't write another pantsuit joke. OKAY! *Women make mistakes.*

All women are different! Some might go in for extreme ironing, or toy voyag-ing. Others might practice Hikaru Dorodango — rolling mud into a small ball. Some collect WWII DeHavilland Mosquito planes. Registered Democrats iden-tifying as female become passionate, profoundly mediocre yoga instructors at age 46. It's the law. Vegetarian women are great in bed. But veegans won't eat anything with a face. Too bad, because us veegans are HOT. I am not really a veegan. I lied again!

Typical. Also, some ladies can't take a joke.

To promote female artists a woman created a website where... "Artists can be searched by ethnicity, religion, and orientation." These included LGBTQ+, Muslim, Hispanic, Asian, African-American, etc.

She invited me to join, but I didn't fill in her questionnaire. I e-mailed her jpegs of my brilliant genius paintings, with a note saying, "Sorry I couldn't fill in your form, but wanted to say I came out on valentines day, 2014 as a BIKE-SEXUAL. I am in love with my own bicycle."

She replied: "As a LGBTQ+* person, I don't get your "joke" - if you join the website, you must respect others.:"

What a humorless twit. I would say humorless cunt, but, As you see, um...I'm not saying that.

And why fit into conventional categories like "Agnostic?"

It's true that female artists are ignored. And artists of color, and LGBTQ+ artists. MOST artists are ignored, and should be! Because we're mostly shite. Have you seen the Whitney Biennial? I rest my case.

..... Old artists are also ignored.

But her form didn't ask "What year were you born?" or "How many Instagram followers do you have?" which amounts to the same thing. Because she's 35. Age isn't her issue.

It's MINE. Self-interest is **human**: I'd tick that box! I am a card-carrying human. And we can carry cards. We have opposable thumbs. I want a human parade! We wipe the floor with those other primates.

And I refuse to check boxes for "Heterosexual" or "Jewish." I'm an open bike-sexual and Involuntary Incel! (don't worry, I'm not going to blow up my high school just because I can't get a poke.)

Also, I have my own faith. I'm a Hamster.

My parents were highly educated, liberal, sophisticated nincompoops. When I was three, my hamster died. What happens when you die? They lamely explained, "Well -Buddhists believe this, Christians believe that, and we're Jews but not really, because beatniks don't believe in God." Also, they told me about sex when I was six. Clearly, they confused me, because then I became a vegetarian.

The point is, you cannot explain the finer points of spirituality to a three-year-old! I needed to believe in a benign power protecting all hamsters, and me, forever, and still do. Hamsterism!

I respect the rights of LGBTQ+ people, but Branding PRIDE has ruined STRIPES and COLORS! ...things I care about. In Iceland, I saw a huge rainbow over a spectacular waterfall, and all I could think was ---"it's so gay!"
We should all be proud of ourselves no matter how despicable we are. But Rainbow Pride Listerine ? SHAME! Now that's an idea I can get behind. I want a SHAME parade. We're all ashamed of something. I'd carry signs saying "I eat cold pizza for BREAKFAST" or "I only wear a bra on special occasions."

===

Ideas like "Let's arm all the school teachers!" are so absurd, but nobody minds the millennial in the "It's the WHITE MEN, STUPID!" T shirt. In a way, she might as well be wearing a KKK hood. To hate people because they grow up to be ignorant assholes is a privilege, a joy, and an excellent hobby. But to hate or blame anybody for what they are born with, or who they love, is obscene.

In Russia, I went to an exhibition of paintings banned during Stalin's Purges, including one called "My Dog, Spot." This is dissident art? Oh yes! Artists not doing Socialist Realism were usually murdered. Artwork had to be political. Personal is so ....bourgeoise.

Who needs Stalin? Our fascism is coming from other NPR supporters!

Now, all artistic expression MUST address race, gender, and the climate crisis. Serious issues. But I don't want to be serious. My nom de plume is jolie-laide balloon! And What's the preferred gender pronoun for "bumblebee pirate clown?" When I find out I'm signing my e-mails with that.

Even with our fabulous opposable thumbs, all homo sapiens are deplorable. You don't see wallabies going around raping! Have you been touched inappro-priately by an Impala? Sexually harassed by a Hippopotamus? I didn't think so.

No Snow Leopard has described African countries as "shitholes." No Killer Whale has called Mexicans "rapists;" And no Koala put that sick-minded bigot in the white house. MEN and WOMEN did.

Oh, Snowball. The sheep are bleating, Again.
"Four legs good, two legs bad!"

"Women good! Men bad!"

If everybody can just relax and enjoy the idea that women are wearing the pants, everybody may get lucky, and nobody will be wearing any pants. Now come with me to the conservatory. I want to show you something.

LAURIE ROSENWALD 2020
##

Rainmaking

Art by Raman Bhardwaj
Poetry by Arien Reed

See, when you're this close to shattering, you sew
yourself together and call it *love*. Only as weak
as your weakest seam, you punch the steel
through skin again because really, you wanted
to unravel. You hem your words back
into your throat and double up the thread
until what echoes back when you sing
to the crows is a tune that infests your bones.
You can dance to this tune and call it *holy*
and mistake the rain for threads of its own.
You can pray to spiraling birds, spiraling stitches,
spiraling feet in mud and *home*, because you're told
God is in everything, even the echoes, but your ears
are double-stitched, for how better to tightly hold
in the scraping tenor of the crows? In the black flashes
of their feathers you see water, earth, and the fire
of *alone*. Even your eyes are a quilted patchwork of
dying embers and undying hurt, or so said the liar
who loosened the cold ribbons of your hair, *precious
as Rumpelstiltskin's straw*, but not his gold.
Your blood is sacred, scarlet thread, your skin is silk
drawn tight, so of course you dance on rain-bruised stones
and tell everyone you're all right. After all, you saw God
tonight in rain, stitches, and the harsh honesty of crows,
and placed every ounce of love for yourself into needles
and dancing bones.

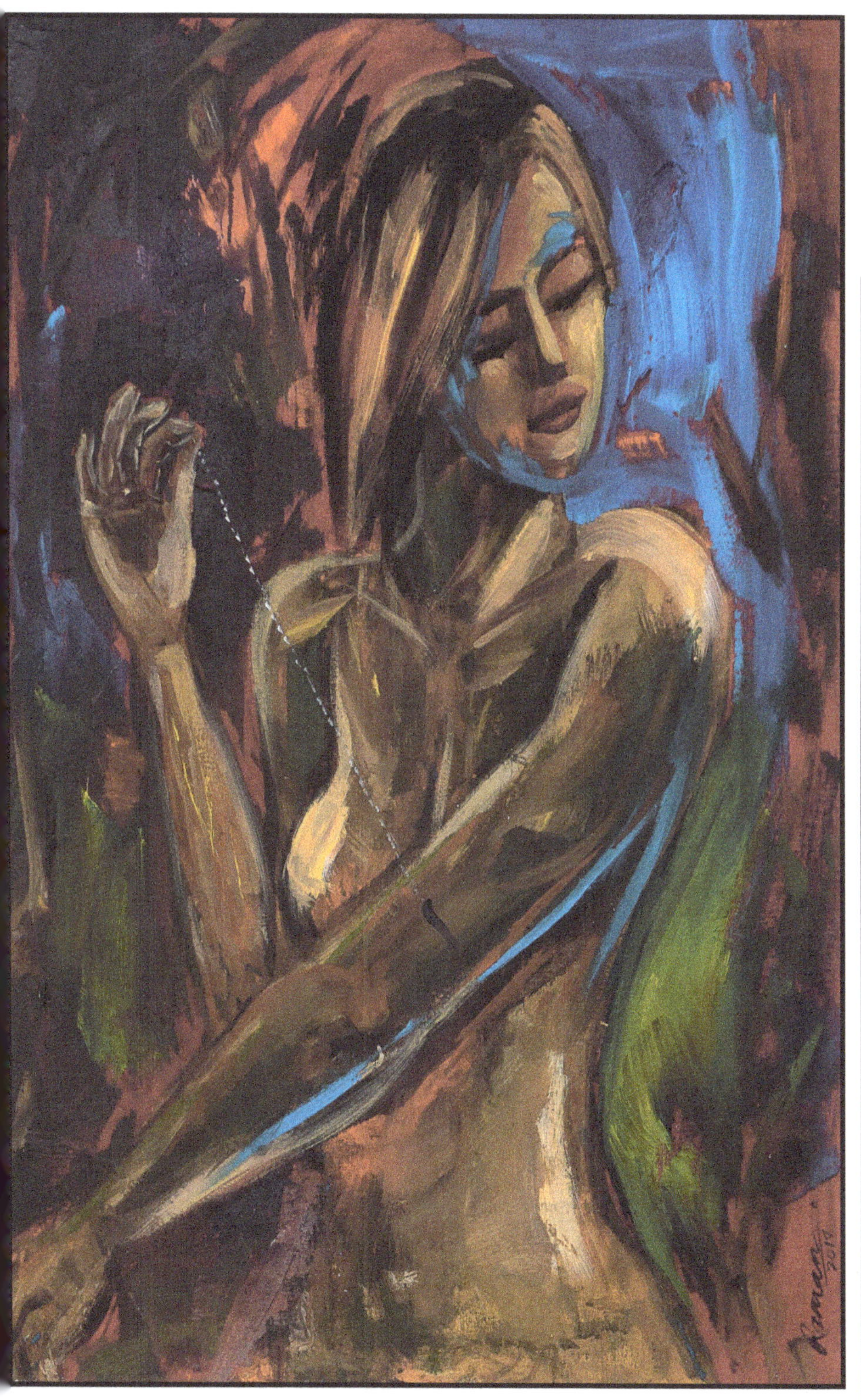

In Order Of Appearance:

Alfredo Arevalo is a queer Chicano writer from Fresno, California. He earned his BA in English (Creative Writing) from the University of Southern California in 2018, where he received the Jimmy Gauntt Memorial Award. He will attend the University of Alabama beginning this fall as a McNair Fellow in the MFA Create Writing program. He loves to explore different genres and styles and, beyond writing, loves to dance, cook, and act.

Nisha Patel is an award-winning queer poet & artist. She is the City of Edmonton's Poet Laureate, and the Canadian Individual Slam Champion. Her debut collection is forthcoming with Newest Press. @anothernisha

Vijay R. Nathan is a supervising librarian and host of the LIVE talk show 'The Truth to Power Show' that streams online on Radio Free Brooklyn. He published two poetry collections including 'Escape from Samsara' (2016) and 'Celebrity Sadhana, Or How to Meditate with a Hammer' (2018), book 1 of the Paparazzo Poet Meditations that imagines meditative moments in celebrity lives. Has been previously published with Newtown Literary, Oddball Magazine, Meow Meow Pow Pow Lit, and Fearsome Critters.

Originally from a small town in British Columbia, Brandon Edwards immigrated to Australia in 2013 and now makes his home in Devonport in North West Tasmania. Brandon's instinct for combining the technical and the creative initially led to a career as a musician and award-winning audio engineer but over the last two decades, Brandon has maintained a dedicated photography practice with a strong observational style that responds to the serendipitous properties of light and movement. His work has appeared in ArtAscent and The Aesthetic Apostle, and has been exhibited in both group and solo shows and private collections in Canada and Australia.

Abigail Markov has been a working studio artist in a diverse range of media for over 15 years. Markov attended the University of Texas at Austin, studying biochemistry, nutrition, sociology, and kinesiology. Their studies were cut short by an unexpected pregnancy and more than 8 years of life as Air Force spouse - including three and a half years overseas. Markov took additional classes in psychology, philosophy, digital art, and video game design, while raising three children, including one with severe behavioral challenges.
Through a divorce, remarriage, and spouse with cancer, Markov has maintained an active, expansive, studio practice, and shown work in a range of small independent galleries and juried shows across Florida and Arizona. Abigail participates as frequently as possible in shows and auctions with ArtCan, a London-based non-profit art organization. Markov has also shown with the International Society of Experimental Artists, Sarasota Art Center, and won an Award of Excellence at the Lake Wales Inaugural Juried Fine Art Show in 2019, awarded by juror Osubi Craig. Abigail now lives and works on a 7.5 acre farm in rural Central Florida with their husband, three fantastic teenagers, and entirely too many chickens.
Instagram: @AbigailMarkov

Laura is a queer Cajun artist and writer from southern Louisiana. Her work has appeared in Mudfish Magazine and the Grief Diaries. She lives in New York. Follow her on instagram @LC.go

Michael Hill's poems have appeared or are forthcoming in Midwestern Gothic, Concho River Review, Third Wednesday, Gray's Sporting Journal, Opossum, Soundings East and other fine publications. He grew up in Western Wisconsin and currently lives in Northern Colorado.

A. Pikovsky is a Philly poet who is the child of Soviet-Jewish immigrants. @little_windmil

Nikolai Sergei Razumov is a transgender artist and writer from Washington D.C. He primarily works with traditional media and writes in the horror and fantasy genres. Nikolai is currently working on the first volume of a collection of short horror stories. He draws inspiration from nature, literature,

nd music and he hopes to present different or unusual perspectives in his artwork.
https://www.instagram.com/duskbatsdrakes

Elizabeth Brewster Thomas's poems have appeared in Poet Lore, The Paris Review (two of which
were chosen for Choice Magazine Listening), Nimrod, Fugue, Southern Poetry Review, The Decadent
Review, Many Mountains Moving, Sow's Ear Poetry Review, Haight Ashbury Literary Journal, The
Sunflower Anthology, and other publications. She received two Academy of American Poets Prizes
while earning her Ph.D. in Creative Writing and Rhetoric from the University of Missouri. Other
awards received include an International Merit Award for Poetry from the Atlantic Review, third
place in The World Monuments Fund Haiku Contest, and finalist placing in the Pablo Neruda Prize
for Poetry, Fugue Poetry Prize, and the New Millennium Writing Award for Poetry. She lives with her
husband and daughter in Columbia, Missouri.

Elidio La Torre Lagares looks after the mineral and the material correspondences with the spiritual/
emotional world, where the poetic image serves as a bridge between both. The lack of capitalization
and punctuation responds to the overall effort of making the poems look like interjections within a
train of thought, a unity with no beginning and no end.
La Torre Lagares earned his MFA in Creative Writing at the University of Texas-El Paso. His work has
appeared in Revista Centro Journal (City University of New York), Azahares (University of Arkan-
sas-Fort Smith), Sargasso (University of Puerto Rico), The Acentos Review, Nagari, Malpaís Review,
The Pigeon Box, New Limestone Review, and The American Poetry Journal.
In 2019, he published «Wonderful Wasteland and other natural disasters» in the New Voices Poetry &
Prose of the University Press of Kentucky.

Lon Hodge is a disabled veteran and retired professor of creative writing. He holds an MFA from
Vermont College.
He has won fellowships from the NEA, Texas Commission on Arts and Humanities and others.
He is widely published and anthologized and is now working on a nonfiction work about travels
across America with a canine bodhisattva.

R. J. Keeler was born in St. Paul, Minnesota, and grew up in the jungles of Colombia. He holds a BS in
Mathematics from North Carolina State University, an MS in Computer Science from the University
of North Carolina-Chapel Hill, an MBA from the University of California at Los Angeles, and a Certif-
icate in Poetry from the University of Washington. An Honorman in the U.S. Naval Submarine School,
he was Submarine Service (SS) qualified. He is a recipient of the Vietnam Service Medal, Honorable
Discharge, and a Whiting Foundation Experimental Grant. He is a member of IEEE (technological
society), AAAS (scientific society), and the Academy of American Poets. A former Boeing engineer.

Julie Blankenship creates archive-inspired, photo-based, mixed media works, exploring history and
the changeable nature of identity. She's obsessed with the object-ness of photographs, working di-
rectly on small, found, black and white photographs that are over 150 years old—hand-altering them
by drawing, abrading, cutting, collaging and layering the images with ink, dust and glue. She digitally
enlarges these works to make 25x40" archival prints.
Blankenship's art is featured on the cover of Of One Free Will, published by Egaeus Press in a limited
edition of a quality of ornateness rarely seen in modern books. Her work was also recently published
in the London Reader and Foxhole Magazine in London, England; and Blood Bath magazine in Edin-
burgh, Scotland. Her work has been exhibited internationally, including solo shows and projects at
Amsterdam Center for Photography, Netherlands; American Institute of Architects, Walter/McBean
Gallery and The Lab Gallery in San Francisco; and group shows at Korean Culture and Arts Foun-
dation in Seoul, Korea; Poorthuis Openluchtmuseum in Genk, Belgium and Center for Photography
International in Haarlem, Netherlands.
She has an MFA from the San Francisco Art Institute, where she later taught photography and inter-
disciplinary art. As Executive Director of Visual Aid, a social justice/arts organization supporting the
creative work of artists with AIDS, Blankenship founded Visual Aid Gallery and curated exhibitions
at many venues. She was recently chosen to participate in Twirl, a new project that will follow the art
making process and studio practice of a group of artists through annual interviews over a decade.
She lives and works in San Francisco, California.

#gillianloop_the_art_of
Gillian began her education as an art major but a naïve fear of poverty lead to a career in fashion comprised not only of form and construction but logo, textile and storyboard design.
In the wake of NAFTA's effect on the garment trade, Gillian established a career in technology, initially in sales and eventually as a project manager. She continued to create art and was awarded ribbons in local fairs, however 2018 marked the start of an explicit art career.
Textile design informs her work utilizing printed elements derived from labels, packaging and magazines to create typically irreverent but sometimes earnest artwork. However a dual perspective; one detailed and the other a more generalized image or theme is consistently evident.

Leon is an avid reader and aspiring writer of poetry. He has published in the Raw Art Review, Prometheus Dreaming, Rumble Fish Quarterly and Cathexis Northwest Press. Leon has a book of poetry, The Uninvented Ear, coming out with UnCollected Press in the Fall of 2020.

Jean Fineberg is a poet and jazz musician with an M.Ed. in Psychology. Her father left a new poem of his every on the table every morning, which was probably Jean's greatest writing catalyst. She recently unearthed a book of poems she wrote when she was eight years old.
Jean grew up with a dictionary on the dinner table. More often than not, she was asked to look up a word.
The omnipresent misuse of correct English, particularly on network television news, has driven her to write this poem. The writing thereof helped relieve her frustration, albeit just temporarily.
Jean has studied with noted poet Kim Addonizio, and her work has been published in Soliloquies Anthology, Vita Brevis, Uppagus and Literary Yard.
She has received seven residency fellowships at art centers around the USA, where she alternates between writing poetry and composing music.

S Akhtar is a London based poet and playwright. They are interested in the intersection of madness and spirituality. They particularly focus on Abrahamic religions, psychosis and addiction.

Amanda's work is inspired by personal experiences as well as the exploration of the feminine experience. With a strong background in photography and Photoshop her images tell a story encompassing many facets of a woman's journey, heart and soul.
Amanda owns Amanda McNeal Photography and currently resides in Franklin, TN with her husband two daughters and fur-baby Flower. In her spare time she enjoys solo-traveling, writing, yoga and gardening.
Artist Portfolio
https://amcneal712.wixsite.com/amandamcneal

Sadie Hoagland has a PhD in fiction from the University of Utah and an MA in Creative Writing/Fiction from UC Davis. Her short story collection, American Grief in Four Stages came out in 2019. Her work has appeared in The Alice Blue Review, The Black Herald, Mikrokosmos Journal, South Dakota Review, Sakura Review, Grist Journal, Oyez Review, Passages North, Five Points, The Fabulist and elsewhere. She is a former editor of Quarterly West, and currently teaches fiction at the University of Louisiana at Lafayette. Her work can be read at sadiehoagland.com

Andrea Jefferson is a writer residing in Southern Louisiana with her lover and cat. She's an editor-at-large for Trampset Magazine and has been featured in Midnight & Indigo, Dying Dahlia Review, Literary Orphans, and others. She can be found on Twitter @honeydreee and Instagram @ biggitybabe.

LAURIE ROSENWALD is a painter, author, humorist, and principal of rosenworld, a design, illustration and animation studio. Actually there is no studio, Miss Rosenwald usually works alone, and rosenworld doesn't exist. In spite of this, rosenworld.com was launched in 1995. Laurie also does humor writing, and writing which is only marginally funny. She's done many, many drawings for The New Yorker magazine, The New York Times, and other fine publications. She collaborated with author David Sedaris on a hilarious app, "David's Diary. Her most recent book is titled "all the wrong people have self-esteem" and is published by Bloomsbury. It is an inappropriate book for young ladies, and frankly, anybody else. Her New York Notebook is on sale at the George Pompidou Center in Paris, and her children's book, And To Name But Just a Few: Red, Yellow, Green, Blue was named a

Scholastic Parent & Child Best Book. It is the only book your family will ever need.
-Laurie has had solo painting exhibitions at SPRING/BREAK ART FAIR 2020, curated by JOHN CHEIM, Galerie Pixi in Paris, among others. She paints with hot, colored wax. In other words, encaustic- a sadly misunderstood medium, much misused by hobbyists and amateurs- anyone who enjoys the smell of burning flesh. She divides her time between New York and Sweden, because she wants to have her cake, eat it too, and then she wants more cake. She speaks Swedish like a native New Yorker, and appeared as "Woman" on "The Sopranos," a role she was born to play. She can draw circles around other people that can draw circles, and claims to have won all the usual awards.

Raman Bhardwaj is a transplant freelance artist. He was born in India and has been living in Greensboro since 2018. He creates murals, canvas art, book illustrations, sometimes sculptures and multimedia works. He won a national award in India for illustrating a children book. He has also won Artpop Street gallery award 2019 in USA. He is a laidback guy who listens to Indian classical music and cooks chicken soup for his soul and is a homeopathy and Astrology enthusiast.

Arien Reed, a queer, trans troublemaker, holds an MFA from National University, lives with his husband, and works at Fresno City College, where he co-founded the LGBTQ Allied Staff and Faculty Association on which he currently serves as president. His poetry and art has appeared, or is forthcoming, in Hippocrates, What Rough Beast, Unlimited Literature, Common Ground Review, TulipTree Review, La Piccioletta Barca, Beyond Words, Infinity Room, Flumes, J Mane Gallery, and others. His troublemaking can be followed on instagram @arienreed or on facebook at facebook.com/arienareed

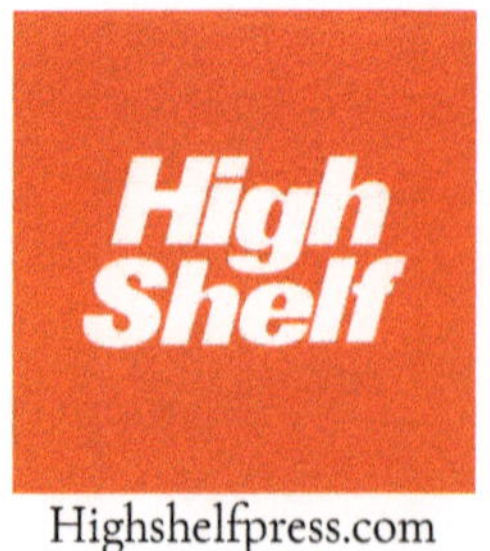

Highshelfpress.com